_f_**P**

To: Tom Innes

Best wishes
Will miss you. you are
an integral part of Intel

Andy 12/99

CREATING THE DIGITAL FUTURE

ALBERT YU

The secrets of

consistent innovation at Intel

THE FREE PRESS *NEW YORK LONDON TORONTO*

SINGAPORE SYDNEY

THE FREE PRESS
A Division of Simon & Schuster Inc.
1230 Avenue of the Americas
New York, NY 10020

THE FREE PRESS and colophon are trademarks
of Simon & Schuster Inc.

Designed by Carla Bolte

Manufactured in the United States of America

10 9 8 7 6 5 4 3 2 1

Library of Congress Cataloging–in–Publicatin Data

Yu, Albert
Creating the digital future : the secrets of consistent innovation
at Intel / Albert Yu.
p. cm.
Includes bibliographical references and index.
ISBN 0–684–83988–1
1. Intel Corporation.   2. Semiconductor industry—United States.
3. Intel microprocessors—United States.   4. High technology
industries—United States—Management.   5. Corporations—United
States.   6. Success in business—United States.   I. Title.
HD9696.S44Y82   1998
338.7'621395'0973—dc21   98-7542
                                                            CIP

CONTENTS

PREFACE

INTEL CORPORATION, OF SANTA CLARA, CALIFORNIA, IS THE WORLD'S largest producer of microprocessors, the "brains" of PCs. The company was founded in 1968 by Gordon Moore, Robert Noyce, and Andy Grove to pursue the business of "integrated electronics," hence the name Intel. The company's first product, the 3101, introduced in 1969, was a 64-bit semiconductor memory device. Today's computer memory chip holds 64 million bits, a million times more than that first semiconductor device 30 years earlier. One year later, Intel came out with a second product, the 1103, with 1,024 bits—16 times more capacity than its first product. The 1103 became an instant success with computer companies as it was cheaper and better than the core memories that it replaced. The 1103 launched a brand new industry: the semiconductor memory industry, which grew rapidly from nothing to about $40 billion in 1997. It also propelled Intel from a startup to a successful company by the early 1970s.

In quick succession, Intel invented another new technology— the world's first microprocessor, the 4004—in 1971. Early microprocessors were used in many digital applications, such as industrial controls, traffic lights, and calculators. The 8080 microprocessor introduced in 1974 was another pivotal product that gave birth to two new industries: microprocessors and personal computers (PCs). Those two businesses grew rapidly to about $50 billion and $250 billion, respectively, by 1997. These products are the basis of the digital revolution unfolding in front of us. Today, microprocessors and PCs are everywhere. Cars, cell phones, pagers, microwave ovens, and most other appliances are more intelligent and useful because of the microprocessors in them. We use networked PCs in our offices to write memos and letters, do financial analysis, make engineering designs, send and receive electronic mail, search and gather information from various databases, and roam the World Wide Web. We're starting to conduct electronic commerce directly from our desktop and mobile PCs. Digital TVs are just around the corner. Digital cameras and printers are poised to replace the conventional analog photography and films.

The digital revolution is a worldwide phenomenon, growing way beyond the United States to include Europe, Japan, and emerging markets in Asia, South America, and Eastern Europe. The excitement over PCs is well exemplified by the "electronic street" in Beijing, China. Extending for several city blocks, this vibrant marketplace contains many small shops selling chips, PCs, and PC accessories. Shopkeepers carry the latest microprocessor chips and can configure systems for customers on the spot. Internet service providers offer instant Internet service for a modest fee. PCs now offer to the people in China and around the world access to instant information worldwide and the ability to communicate with others via the Internet. These merchants used to sell food, clothing, and other household goods, but they switched to selling digital products as the demand soared.

The Intel marketing team in Beijing experimented in 1996 with a novel street bazaar one weekend selling chips and PCs. Several blocks of the electronic street were set up for foot traffic only. Merchants put on specials. People showed up with their families and friends to see new products and shop. Intel hired many university students to put on caps and gowns labeled "PC Doctor" and talk about PC technologies and products. The bazaar was jam-packed with 80,000 people, who bought more than 10,000 PCs and microprocessors in one weekend. Since that successful experiment, this innovative street bazaar idea has been orchestrated in many other emerging markets.

Since the birth of our first microprocessor, Intel has invented and produced nine consecutive generations of successful high-volume microprocessors that have helped to propel the fast-growing PC industry: the 8080, 8086, 80286, 386, 486, Pentium® processor, Pentium® processor with MMX™ technology, Pentium® Pro processor, and most recently the Pentium® II processor. Each new generation has represented a quantum jump in computing capabilities made possible by successive technical breakthroughs. Each new microprocessor generation has also created new business opportunities for many who took advantage of the new computing power to bring great new digital products and services to market.

How did we create so many successes—and yet some notable failures? We have worked hard to establish clear strategies and action plans to deliver compelling products. We try to learn continuously from our own and others' successes and mistakes. We aim to improve and learn constantly. In this book, I hope to share what we at Intel have learned about defining, developing, and delivering winning high-technology products that have fueled the digital revolution, generation after generation. We foster innovation, collaborate with key industry players, and achieve constant organizational learning and operational excellence. This will continue to be essential to creating and managing high-technology digital products of the future. I hope that you'll enjoy reading an inside perspective of microprocessor development at Intel, from the first 4004 microprocessor to the recent Pentium II processor and beyond.

By way of giving you a "map" to the book, Chapter 1 discusses the famous Moore's Law and its implication for the high-technology business. Chapter 2 acquaints the reader with the early days of the microprocessor and the PC. Chapters 3 through 7 look at some of Intel's key strategic and operational management principles and practices. Chapters 8 through 12 show these principles in action, through inside stories about Intel's development of the 386, the 486, the Pentium processor, and beyond.

ACKNOWLEDGMENTS

THIS BOOK IS BASED ON THE MANY YEARS I HAVE SPENT MANAGING high-technology products and business at Intel Corporation. I would like to acknowledge and thank Andy Grove, Intel's Chairman, for setting the direction and the tone of the Intel management system right from the company's earliest days. Andy not only pushes the state of the art in high-technology management to new heights every day, but he has been an inspirational teacher and mentor to many. I would also like to thank many of my colleagues at Intel and in the PC industry around the world from whom I have learned a great deal over the years.

This book benefited significantly from the constant encouragement and thoughtful suggestions of Robert Wallace of The Free Press. I value Robert's contributions greatly. I also would like to thank Jane Glasser who has tirelessly helped me in preparing and refining the manuscript. Last but not least, I would like to acknowledge my wife, Mary Bechmann, who has been a constant source of creative ideas, insights, and support throughout the process.

CHAPTER ONE

PLAN THE
COMPUTING FUTURE

AT THE MICROPROCESSOR FORUM IN SAN JOSE, CALIFORNIA, ON October 14, 1997, in front of 1,200 key players in the microprocessor and personal computer industry, top Intel architect John Crawford and his colleague at Hewlett-Packard unveiled the future of computing. A totally captivated standing-room-only audience learned for the first time the technical details of the new EPIC[1] technology for Intel's upcoming 64-bit microprocessor product line. Several microprocessors incorporating this technology are under development, and the first product, code-named Merced™, is expected to be on the market by the turn of the century. Merced was labeled the "Killer Chip" by *Fortune* magazine.[2] These 64-bit microprocessors represent the next giant leap in performance and capability that will allow the microprocessors to power the full spectrum of computing from its current base of personal computers to mainframes, supercomputers, and beyond. Several leading companies such as Microsoft, Hewlett-Packard, Compaq, IBM, and Sequent presented their respective software and hardware product plans to take full advantage of the power of the Merced chip. In addition to the 64-bit disclosure, Fred Pollack, Intel's head of microprocessor planning, detailed our complete microprocessor product road map, including both the 32-bit and the 64-bit products, all the way out to the year 2001. How do we plan and develop our product road maps so far into the future?

What are the technological and economic trends for the future of digital products? What does computing look like into the next millennium?

MICRO 2001

Charles F. Kettering, former director of research at General Motors, once said, "I am interested in the future, because I have to spend the rest of my life there." My key managers and I spend lots of time planning future generations of microprocessors. No matter how good a processor Intel has just introduced, the next one—usually the next two—are well underway, and that's where our attention is focused. In 1988, three Intel colleagues and I mapped out our view of what the leading microprocessor would be in the year 2001, and called it Micro 2001.[3] We predicted that the leading-edge microprocessor would have nine million transistors on a chip by 1997 and 100 million by 2001, due to silicon technology advances. We were close: the Intel Pentium II processor in 1997 has over eight million transistors, and I believe that we are well on our way to making the 100-million-transistor microprocessor a reality by 2001. In addition, we projected that the microprocessor of 1997 would perform eight times faster than the 486, based on the increased transistor count. The actual Pentium II processor performance turns out to be a lot higher: about 25 times faster than the 486. Clearly there has been an enormous amount of innovation in computer architecture over the last few years that we did not foresee in 1989. This includes the concepts of dynamic execution, a novel idea that speeds up microprocessor performance, and the Dual Independent Bus, both of which are featured in the Pentium II processor and will be described in more detail later. From 1997 to 2001, microprocessor performance is expected to increase by another factor of 10. When we published our projections in 1989, many people thought we were being too optimistic. It turned out that our forecasted performance jumps were way too conservative!

MOORE'S LAW REIGNS

How could we predict in 1988 the enormous increase in the number of transistors that could be placed on a chip by 2001? In 1965,[4] back in the early days of silicon integrated circuits, Gordon Moore, one of Intel's founders and then head of Fairchild Semiconductor Research and Development Laboratory, set forth a principle concerning the pace of semiconductor advances that has since become known as Moore's Law. This "law" states that the number of transistors on a semiconductor chip doubles approximately every 18 to 24 months. For microprocessors, the doubling of transistors has occurred about every 24 months, as shown in Figure 1. This simple statement, one of the most significant in the semiconductor industry, has held true since 1965 and promises to be a good predictor for semiconductor advances well into the twenty-first century. Now chairman emeritus of Intel, Gordon has been the industry's visionary for decades. He is an unassuming man with incredible insights on technology and business. At meetings he usually sits quietly listening to various discussions and

FIGURE 1   MOORE'S LAW (TO 1998)

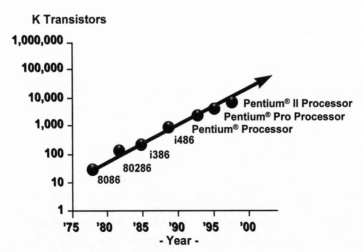

Source: Intel

arguments until suddenly he comes up with a clear and crisp statement that hits at the heart of a matter and establishes a guiding principle. When Gordon speaks, everyone listens.

Let me explain how Moore's Law came about and what it means. One of the most significant inventions of the twentieth century—before the microprocessor—was the integrated circuit. Integrated circuit technology made the semiconductor memory and microprocessor possible. Robert Noyce, another founder of Intel, helped invent the integrated circuit at Fairchild Semiconductor in 1957. Noyce discovered that instead of hooking up individual transistors to build an electronic circuit, it was possible to build the whole circuit on a single chip of silicon by connecting the various elements, such as transistors, capacitors, and resistors, with aluminum interconnections on the chip itself. As the circuitry was all integrated on a single chip, it was called an integrated circuit, or IC. The benefits were immediately apparent. A single IC package could replace an entire circuit board, saving space. It was much more reliable and cost far less than the board. The ability to build complex electronics functions on a single piece of silicon was a major technological breakthrough and became the foundation of semiconductor memories and microprocessors that have fueled the digital explosion.

THE MIRACLE OF SILICON

It is the unique electrical and chemical properties of silicon—silicon dioxide and thin aluminum layers—that make possible the dynamics of Moore's Law. It turns out that as one builds smaller MOS (metal oxide simiconductor) transistors in silicon, the transistors perform faster and consume less power. Silicon dioxide is a perfect insulator because, as it gets thinner for smaller devices, it continues to perform predictably and reliably. Aluminum[5] is a perfect conductor to form electrical connections; it just happens to stick to silicon and silicon dioxide really well to form very reliable interconnections. The combined properties of these elements make the ever-shrinking transistor and more complex integrated circuits possible.

I know of no other technology that gets better as the element gets smaller. For example, neither internal combustion engines nor electric motors get better as they get smaller. The miracle of silicon provides the foundation for the whole high-technology industry. This new industry grew rapidly from 1957, and Fairchild Semiconductor was one of its leaders.

As silicon technology advances and transistors get smaller, more of them can be packed on a single chip to perform more complex electronics functions. For example, let's say the next generation of silicon technology allows us to pack 2,000 transistors on a single chip, instead of the maximum of 1,000 that we could place in the previous generation. What happens? First of all, one can build a 1,000-transistor chip on the new technology that is half the size of the previous-generation chip. Because the cost of a chip is roughly proportional to its size, the new chip will cost only about half what

FIGURE 2   EIGHT-INCH SILICON WAFER

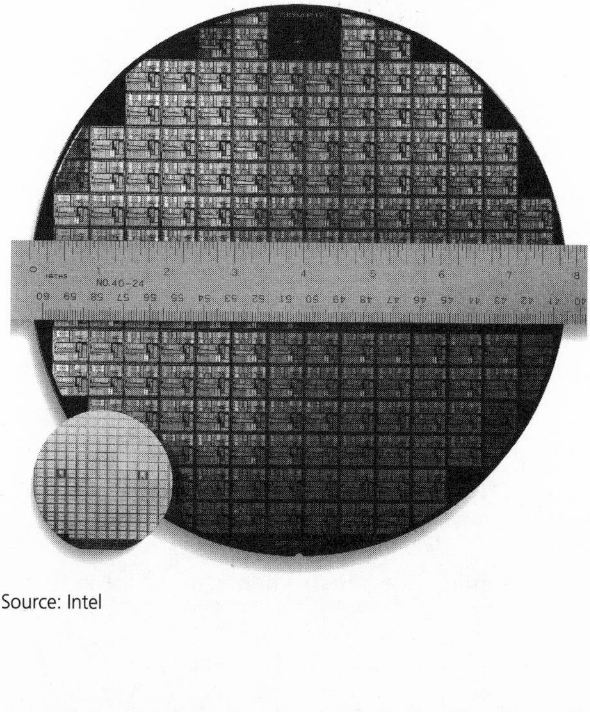

Source: Intel

the old chip costs. In addition, the smaller chip will perform at higher speeds and consume less power. Therefore, it can be sold for less than the old chip, while performing better in every way! This clearly is more attractive to customers; more people buy the chip, and the volume grows rapidly. But that's not all. With the new technology offering 2,000 transistors per chip, engineers have twice as much freedom to implement new product ideas that were simply not feasible with the old technology. In fact, this is exactly what happened with the first microprocessor, the Intel 4004, which required about 2,000 transistors to implement the needed functions. It simply was not possible with the previous generation of technology.

In summary, there are two major benefits of shrinking transistors: (1) companies can offer current products at higher performance and lower cost, and (2) engineers can create new products that were not possible before. These two benefits have been the driving forces of the runaway success of semiconductor products. As the business grows and generates more profits, more money can be spent on research and development to create the next generation of silicon technology which, in turn, allows better, cheaper, and more powerful products to be developed. And the cycle just keeps repeating. This is the essence of Moore's Law.

Why 18 to 24 months? That is typically the time it takes in our highly competitive environment to develop new technology and new products. The development process usually consists of defining the product/technology specification with customer feedback (3 months), developing the product/technology with teams of highly specialized talent (12 to 18 months), and getting the product/technology into production and the marketplace (3 months). Should the competitive intensity lessen, the pace of development may slow. Conversely, as competition picks up, the pace may accelerate. Over the last 30 years or so, the doubling of transistors on a single chip every 18–24 months has been the average pace of semiconductor advances.

Companies such as Fairchild, Texas Instruments, and Motorola became early leaders of the semiconductor IC industry by aggressively driving the pace of development according to Moore's Law. The IC business has grown enormously, and today it is truly global, with major players like NEC, Toshiba, and Samsung, in addition to Intel, Motorola, and others.

As interest in high technology has grown, Moore's Law has been mentioned frequently in the press and in articles. Many people today argue that Moore's Law will not hold in the future. Some point out that the use of far-ultraviolet light to define even smaller line widths, new metal interconnects such as copper, and novel schemes to increase storage in memory cells will cause semiconductor advances to occur faster than what Moore's Law predicts. Others argue that the increased power consumption of chips, escalating capital outlay needed for semiconductor manufacturing, and the demand for lower-cost chips will cause advances to occur more slowly. Both sides of the argument may be valid. Looking back, we have always encountered many technical and business barriers in advancing the technology. However, the industry keeps coming up with ingenious and innovative solutions to keep the advances going. This will continue in the future. I believe that Moore's Law will hold well into the next millennium.

THE BUSINESS IMPLICATIONS OF MOORE'S LAW

What are the consequences of Moore's Law? First, it predicts the pace at which silicon technology and products will advance—a doubling of capabilities every 18–24 months. This means that electronics functions will increase by a factor of about 10 in 6.6 years, a factor of 100 in 13 years, a factor of 1,000 in 20 years! New products with increasing capabilities will be available in the marketplace at an increasingly rapid pace. If your products are improving at a slower pace than predicted by Moore's Law, you can bet that other companies will outrun you. A clear consequence of this law is that if you rest on your laurels, you will be rendered obsolete by your competition. You must obsolete your own products or others will do it for you. There is an old Chinese saying: "In going upstream, if you don't advance, you automatically fall behind."

The second consequence of Moore's Law is that as the cost of ICs drops continuously with ever-advancing silicon technologies, new pricing strategies are necessary. Companies have two choices. They can continue charging the same prices and hope to reap larger profits. But this works only in an environment with little competition. Or, they can drop prices to attract more buyers and hope to reap even more profits as the volume rises faster than the price drops. In fact, that is what has happened in the semiconductor business: the market has expanded much faster than prices have dropped. As the market grows and revenues increase, profits can be plowed back into developing new technologies and more new products, which fuel market growth even further. Again, the cycle continues. This business dynamic is totally different than for industries in which the technology advances more slowly.

The third consequence of Moore's Law is that one must drive to deliver higher and higher volume to expand the market. In the high-tech business, volume is everything. If one does not have enough manufacturing capacity, competitors will come in and take the business away. At the same time, state-of-the-art manufacturing facilities for leading-edge technology are extremely expensive: it cost more than $2 billion to build a high-volume wafer fabrication facility in 1997. Therefore, it is essential that the factory is fully loaded with the right products. This task of building the right amount of capacity, at the right time, with the right product mix, is at the heart of running a successful semiconductor business.

THE SOFTWARE IMPLICATIONS OF MOORE'S LAW

Moore's Law also drives the pace of software advances and business strategy. When computing-hardware performance improves slowly and the number of computers in use is small, as in the days of mainframes, the appropriate software strategy is to charge high prices for each piece of software sold and to deliver more functionality and performance in software products by rewriting the software code. This was what happened during the mainframe era. However, when computing power doubles every two years and millions of computers are being shipped every day, as the PC world follows Moore's Law, the software strategy must be different. Existing software runs better on the next faster microprocessors. There is no need to rewrite the code. An example is Microsoft Windows® 3.0, which ran poorly on a 386 processor-based PC but great on a 486 processor–based system. This was what drove the popularity of Windows 3.0 and 486-based PCs. Thus, there is no need for software companies to fine-tune their existing software for better performance. The next generation of microprocessors will do that for them, faster and cheaper.

Instead, software developers must move forward to create new classes of software for new markets, by taking full advantage of the faster computers that Moore's Law predicts are just around the corner. A good example is Intel's Pentium processor with MMX™ technology. This product has new technology built in to enable software developers to create new and faster multimedia applications. Many forward-looking software companies like Microsoft, Adobe, Macromedia, and others, knowing that this new product was coming, devoted resources to generate new applications that would take advantage of the new technology. When Intel announced the Pentium processor with MMX technology, these companies were ready, with exciting and highly successful new applications for consumers. The market expands. Everyone benefits. Another example is three-dimensional (3D) graphics capabilities. Intel and the hardware industry are building chips with high-performance 3D graphics capabilities at very low cost, by advancing the technology according to Moore's Law. We are bringing expensive, workstation-level graphics performance into PC price points that everybody can afford. Software developers have seized that opportunity and are developing new applications for home and office that deliver appealing and life-like 3D software. The combination will again create exciting new applications that will expand the total market for all of us.

In addition, the software pricing strategy needs to be different in a world that follows Moore's Law. As the number of computers in use is in the hundreds of millions and rising by millions each month, one can generate much higher revenue and profit by selling software at very low prices to attract as many buyers as possible to achieve a high-volume business. This is totally different from selling expensive software in a small mainframe market where the volume is small and stagnant. Therefore, the pace of software development and the business strategy are profoundly affected by Moore's Law.

MICRO 2011: WHAT DOES THE CRYSTAL BALL SAY?

What will the microprocessor be like in the year 2011—on its fortieth anniversary? Armed with Moore's Law, let us try to look into the future.[6] Figure 3 indicates that by the year 2011, the microprocessor will have a mind-boggling one billion transistors! That's a jump of 150 times that of the most advanced chip of 1997, the Pentium II processor. Consider this: if each person represents a transistor, this

FIGURE 3   MOORE'S LAW (TO 2011)

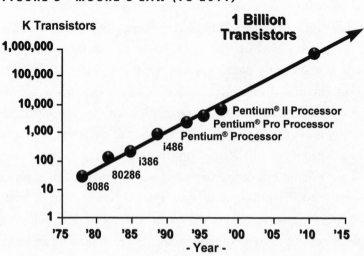

Source: Intel

chip will have over five times the total population of the United States on that little piece of silicon! Its performance will be about 150 times that of the fastest Pentium II processor. From our last experience, we may have underestimated the performance boost again. The new EPIC technology for our Merced chip has tremendous upside potential in performance that may surprise us. There will be many innovative ideas to boost performance and lower the power for future generations of microprocessors. We haven't seen anything yet. The best is yet to come.

Why would anybody want more computing power than we already have? This question has been asked ever since the very first computer was invented. In 1985, when Intel introduced the 32-bit 386 microprocessor, many people said, "My 286 PC is good enough. I don't need more power." However, given more processor power, old software runs much faster and becomes more usable. And more importantly, brand new classes of applications spring up to take advantage of the newfound power.

Looking ahead, I can think of at least five application areas that will take giant leaps ahead with new and more powerful microprocessors. First, we will be able to interface with computers much more intuitively and naturally. We will be able to talk to the computer and use handwriting as inputs. The computer screen will have lifelike three-dimensional graphics along with stereo sound, and it will give us sensory feedback such as movement and vibration. In short, we will be able to interact with the computer much as we would with another person and with real-world objects. This has long been a dream of many people, but it will require enormous computing power and clever software. The new processors coming along, together with innovative software, will make this dream come true.

Second, computers will be our smart and hardworking assistants, getting the information we need, carrying out the tasks we want done, keeping track of our calendars, suggesting activities or decisions based on our past practices or wishes. These capabilities will be welcomed in the office as well as in the home. We do accomplish these time-consuming tasks today, but through a complex and disjointed amalgam of sticky notes, pocket calendars, voice mail, phone, World Wide Web, electronic mail, fax, TV, video, newspapers. With the increased computing power on our desktops and with improved networked server infrastructure around the world, the electronic assistant will be a reality in a few years.

Third, we will have access to information and the ability to conduct business securely—including browsing, buying, and selling around the world 24 hours a day with instant response. This will require very powerful networked servers that are fast and reliable and need little maintenance. These should be connected with super-high-bandwidth networks that will overcome most of the problems of today's Internet, which is slow and unreliable. More powerful microprocessors will allow networked servers not only to run faster but to incorporate self-repair and security features. We need desktop computers that are connected to the network to have natural interfaces, lifelike graphics, and security protection for our use in the office and at home.

Fourth, the digital revolution will indeed reach the home. The home PC is a reality today. As prices drop, people will have multiple PCs at home linked together with the upcoming home network using wireless and power lines and to the high-speed Internet. Digital TV with high-resolution screens will replace analog TV in a few years. With digital capability, the new TV will incorporate many powerful but easy-to-use computing features tailored to consumers.

Lastly, we will carry with us lightweight and wallet-sized computers with long-lasting batteries to use for wireless communication and computing while we travel. The current hand-held devices are hard to use and have limited computing and communications capabilities. Many notebook computers today are heavy, bulky, and have short battery lives. All these new capabilities will be available to us, at relatively low cost, in the near future, due to advances in technology that allow more and more computing power to be packed into smaller and smaller computers that consume very little battery power.

These are just five examples of how more computing power will benefit all of us. They also illustrate the tremendous new business opportunities available to many companies, enabled by the more powerful and lower-cost microprocessors coming in the near future.

The pace of high-technology development is driven by Moore's Law. As silicon technology advances, products get better and cheaper, new classes of product are created, markets expand, revenue and profit increase to fund more development, and the cycle repeats. Moore's Law is not a law of physics but it results from the close interplay between technology and business. The two feed upon one another to enable more advanced products, which creates bigger and bigger markets. As a result, high-technology companies must constantly replace their own products with new ones at the pace of Moore's Law, or they will be left behind. One must constantly look to the future.

CHAPTER TWO

CREATE A
NEW INDUSTRY

THE MICROPROCESSOR ENTERED THE WORLD ALMOST AS AN ACCIDENT.
Most successful products, in fact, result from a combination of intelligent strategy and serendipitous discovery. However, when a fragile new product or idea comes about, how it's nurtured and managed makes all the difference in the world. This is especially true if you are creating a whole new industry with new rules, new opportunities, and new pitfalls.

THE FIRST MICROPROCESSOR: THE 4004 IS BORN

Gordon Moore had always been interested in building a computer on a chip. While at Fairchild Semiconductor R&D, he had led a group doing research in this area. In 1969, a Japanese calculator company called Busicom approached Intel about building custom chips for use in their programmable calculators. Gordon, president of Intel at the time, was not interested in custom products; he wanted Intel to build noncustom products that could be sold in high volume to a variety of customers. But Gordon did not turn the Busicom request down, because Intel was just a startup company anxious to attract new business. The Busicom request might be the opportunity to create such a chip for practical applications. He asked computer scientist Ted Hoff, who did his research work at Stanford and was one of the most creative minds at Intel, to look into how to solve the challenge of meeting Busicom's and Intel's seemingly conflicting needs.

After working on the problem for a while, Ted came up with a novel idea. Instead of designing each calculator chip totally differently, he invented a way to partition the job into two pieces: a general-purpose control logic processor chip and a separate read-only memory (ROM) chip that stored the program specific for the application. For different calculators, only the program and the ROM needed to be different. The same control logic processor chip could be used for all different models of the calculator. In fact, this processor could be used for other digital applications as well. This was a major breakthrough on two levels. On the technical side, the long-wished-for "computer on a chip" was at hand, as the control logic processor chip could be implemented with the integrated circuit technology available at the time on a single chip. On the business side, one set of components could be used for many different applications. This opened up the possibility of producing volume products for many logic applications and many customers. Intel coined the word "microprocessor" for the control logic portion of the chip, for it was, in fact, a micro-processor.

Frederico Faggin, an intense and brilliant Italian engineer who

FIGURE 4   INTEL'S 4004 AD

Source: Intel

had worked on advanced silicon technology at Fairchild in the late '60s, took on the task with a very small team to design the first microprocessor chip. In just nine months, the world's first microprocessor, the 4004, was born. It contained just over 2,000 transistors, which is minuscule by today's standards (the Intel Pentium II processor contains about eight million transistors). It was accompanied by three other components: the 4001 RAM, 4002 ROM, and 4003 register chips. Intel's first microprocessor was introduced in 1971 with the advertising headline, "Announcing a new era of integrated electronics: a microprogrammable computer on a chip!" It was an accurate description.

As exciting as the promise of this new product seemed, few people knew what to do with this rudimentary device other than to build calculators. Compared with minicomputer and mainframe computers that were 16 and 32 bits,[7] the humble 4-bit 4004 ran very slowly and had very limited capabilities. It was immediately clear that an 8-bit processor would run a lot faster and be much more useful. Faggin and his team worked quickly to implement the 8-bit microprocessor, the 8008, which was introduced in 1972. At the time, Intel was producing lots of 1103 memories, and the 8008 was a very low-volume product. It was still a very crude machine and ran slowly. It was useful as a microcontroller that performed many logic control functions but not much else.

BEGINNING OF MICROCOMPUTING: THE 8080

A number of people saw the potential of using the 8008 as a basic computing element. One of the early 8008 enthusiasts was Bill Gates, who was then a teenage programmer using his school's DEC minicomputer. When he and his friend Paul Allen first saw the 8008, they were fascinated by it. They bought a chip, built a single-board computer, and began programming. Allen suggested that they come up with a Basic language for the chip, to make programming easier. Their attempts were unsuccessful, as the 8008 chip was simply not powerful enough.

At the same time, Faggin and his team had figured out how they needed to improve the design to make it a real computer chip. They quickly designed the third microprocessor, the 8080, on a more advanced silicon technology that added more transistors to perform more complex computing functions and to make the chip run faster. Remember Moore's Law? The team worked around the clock to complete this important chip while several other companies like Motorola and Texas Instruments raced to produce a competitive product. Faggin told me at the time that he knew that the 8080 would revolutionize the industry, as he felt the chip had just enough power to be really useful as the brain of a small computer. He was right. It was the 8080, introduced in 1974, that started the PC revolution. The third time proved to be a charm.

In 1975, right after the 8080 was introduced, a small company called MITS, in Albuquerque, New Mexico, built the first microcomputer using the 8080, the Altair 8800. By today's standards, it was a rudimentary machine, but it showed the world for the first time the possibility of a "personal" computer. Gates and Allen immediately bought an Altair microcomputer, and they were able to develop their working Basic language for the 8080. That was the first product from their partnership, which later became the software giant Microsoft. Microsoft Basic became an early standard used by everybody in the microcomputer world. Many people rushed to generate successful software applications using this Basic language. People quickly found that they could use these little computers to do what they had been doing on much more expensive minicomputers and mainframes, and they rushed to buy more. All of a sudden, the microcomputer hardware and software businesses were born.

CREATE A NEW BUSINESS MODEL

With the invention of the first microprocessor in 1971, Intel quickly realized that this exciting new business needed a new business model. In order to sell lots of microprocessors, we had to help our customers to design microprocessor-based systems and boards easily and to create lots of new software applications for these systems. Both the system design and software programming disciplines were new to us in the semiconductor memory business. Ed Gelbach, Intel's vice president of marketing and sales, recruited Bill Davidow, who had been working in computer systems at Hewlett-Packard, to start an operation to build and sell microprocessor development systems, software tools to help our customers create new microprocessor-based applications quickly and efficiently. In addition to recruiting hardware system talents, Davidow also attracted many minicomputer software experts to develop high-level languages such as PL1, FORTRAN, and COBOL on Intel microprocessors, so that Intel's customers could develop their applications based on these efficient languages. We also contracted Gary Kildal of Digital Research to develop an operating system, called ISIS, just for Intel's development systems. Kildal kept the rights to modify ISIS and sold a similar product called CP/M,* which subsequently became the first de facto standard operating system for 8080-based microcomputers.

We sold a lot of these development systems through the 1970s—with the purpose of helping people develop applications for microprocessors—while our microprocessor sales were quite small. At one point, Intel's sales of development systems were so high that we were ranked number seven as a minicomputer company! What was in fact happening was that many customers bought our development systems to use as general-purpose microcomputers. Intel was really the first personal computer company and didn't even realize it! Thinking back, Intel's "blue box," the nickname for our microprocessor development system, was a full-fledged personal computer. We were so busy forming one new industry—microprocessors—that we failed to see another new opportunity right in front of our eyes—personal computers. Intel was so focused on making the microprocessor successful that we viewed the development systems business as supporting cast rather than a potential

*CP/M, UNIX, DOS, Windows NT, etc., are trademarked by their respective companies.

star in its own right. One can always speculate whether Intel would have done as well in microprocessors if it had chased two major new product categories at the same time rather than focusing on one. We'll never know the answer.

"What else do we need to do to accelerate Intel's budding microprocessor business?" Bill Davidow asked himself. To help our customers design their microprocessor-based systems more easily, we needed to supply them with all the necessary support chips. We also needed to give them technical training and support. In short, Intel had to offer its customers "complete products": support chips, development systems, software tools, and technical support, and not just the microprocessor devices.[8] This was a brand-new concept for people in the semiconductor business, as we did not need any of these to sell computer memories. Creating and implementing a new business model to supply "complete products" was clearly taking a risk, because it was very expensive to develop and market these hardware and software products and the appropriate support organizations. On the other hand, the upside was enormous: it was the billions of dollars in the microprocessor business that we were after. It turned out that our strategy worked extremely well. The "complete products" were exactly what our customers needed to quickly build a large number of high-volume microprocessor-based applications. Their businesses grew rapidly. We sold lots of microprocessors. The risk paid off.

MARSHAL THE POWER OF MARKETING

HOW TO WIN THE 16-BIT RACE

Though Intel's 8-bit 8080 microprocessor created an industry, many competitors quickly crowded into the marketplace. First was Zilog, founded by Frederico Faggin who left Intel. Then came Motorola, Texas Instruments, National Semiconductor, and many others. Their 8-bit products competed strongly with ours. Our marketing and engineering resources were consumed by the competitive battle.

In the high-technology business, the winner in one generation of technology seldom becomes the winner in the next. For example, the electronic vacuum tube industry was led by RCA and Raytheon. However, these companies never became big players in the succeeding semiconductor industry, which was led by new players like Texas Instruments, Motorola, and Fairchild. Our competitors moved aggressively to seize the lead of the next round: 16-bit microprocessors, which could run programs faster than 8-bit products. These processors would put microcomputer performance on par with that of 16-bit minicomputers, opening up a giant market. By the mid-1970s, many 16-bit microprocessors from our competitors were on the market before ours: Zilog's Z8000, Motorola's 6800, and several others.

Realizing that we were behind, Les Vadasz, Intel's vice president of engineering at the time, put together a task force to quickly come up with a 16-bit microprocessor. We realized that the 8080 was based on a controller architecture and that the 16-bit machine must be designed to handle more demanding computing needs in the future. One critical product requirement was that Intel's 16-bit machine must be able to run all the 8-bit software written for the 8080, as there was a huge number of these programs around. The concept of *software compatibility* was new at the time, but Intel fortunately understood its significance, and it has become a cornerstone of our microprocessor business strategy since then. Software compatibility offers customers the important assurance of running all existing software on future generations of computers, without expensive software rewrites. This preservation of past software investments represents a huge asset to most companies.

Intel's Bill Pohlman, an energetic engineer, was put in charge of Intel's 16-bit microprocessor development. He and his team worked feverishly to come up with the 16-bit 8086, which was introduced in 1978. A year later, a lower-cost version, the 8088, was introduced. The 8088 was basically an 8086 with an 8-bit bus,[9] which allowed it to work in existing 8-bit boards with existing components. The initial market reaction to both the 8086 and the 8088 was less than enthusiastic. Motorola, Zilog, and National all touted their chips as being better. Adding to the pressure, the fast-growing Apple Computer, Inc., chose the MOS Technology 6502 (which was compatible with the Motorola 6800) as the heart of its very popular Apple II computer. Another PC maker, Commodore, also chose the 6502 for its PET microcomputer. These wins gave the Motorola architecture an early lead in the emerging 16-bit microprocessor marketplace.

THE CRUSH CAMPAIGN

By the fall of 1979, we were very worried about Intel's poor position in the 16-bit market. Bill Davidow urgently pulled together a task force that included Dave House, the marketing manager for microprocessors; Jim Lally, the general manager of board products; Casey Powell, the eastern region sales manager; Regis McKenna, Intel's top PR consultant; and several others. Their job was to brainstorm ideas for winning the 16-bit business. The group worked around the clock and came up with the idea of a major marketing campaign. We had to sell the products that we had. The key was to sell our strengths: a strong image as a technology leader; a complete products offering; a plan for enhancing it; a competent sales force; and excellent service and support organizations. We needed to get this story out to our target audience and do it quickly.

Who was our audience? The answer surprised us. We discovered that three distinct groups of people contributed to the decision of which microprocessor a company would commit to. Engineering was involved, because they were the people who had to design products based on the microprocessors. This was the audience Intel was accustomed to dealing with in our memory business. Purchasing people were involved, because they authorized purchases, not only of microprocessors but of support chips, development system, boards, and software, and these added up to a sizable purchase. We had dealt with purchasing people in the sale of memory products, too. What was new was that CEOs were also usually involved in the microprocessor decision, since the selection of a microprocessor had dramatic long-term strategic implications for the company. This was a new audience for Intel, since CEOs had seldom been involved in the purchase of semiconductor memories. The task force realized that a successful marketing campaign would have to bring Intel's story to all three groups, and particularly to CEOs.

So, the key objective for the task force was to come up with crisp and forceful presentations on Intel's microprocessor strength to address these three different audiences. This important marketing program, named the "Crush" campaign, was the most comprehensive marketing campaign that Intel had ever put together. The goal was nothing short of winning the 16-bit microprocessor race.

In our marketing presentations, we wanted to show that we had a long-term product road map, with a steady supply of better and faster microprocessors. A CEO would want to know Intel's product offering a few years ahead, as his future products would be dependent upon Intel's product road maps. The stronger Intel's future product line, the stronger his own products would be. He also wanted to make sure his selection of Intel microprocessors would preserve his major software and hardware development efforts. The engineering audience needed to see the same road map, but at a greater level of detail: how much better would the next two microprocessors be? Would the support chips satisfy the design needs? How would the next development systems and software make the engineer's job easier? Purchasing managers wanted to see future pricing and volume projections that would give them the assurance that they could get future products at reasonable prices and at desired volume levels. Based on these needs, we tailored our Crush campaign presentations and messages to these three distinct audiences, with sufficient detail to satisfy them all.

How would we measure the success of the Crush campaign in the 16-bit microprocessor race? Without concrete indicators, we would not know whether we were making progress toward our goal. We decided that when a company bought a development system and started a serious engineering effort to design their products with our microprocessors, we would call it a "design win." If a company committed money to buying a development system and committed engineering resources to designing for our microprocessors, there was a good chance that they would develop a new product using our microprocessor and bring that to market. They would then buy microprocessors from us in volume, assuming that their product became a success in the marketplace. So a good early measure of our campaign's success would be the number of "design wins." The team set a very ambitious goal of getting 2,000 "design wins" by the end of the first year, 1980.

The task force pulled together the marketing presentations and messages, processor product road maps, complete solution details, and many other materials in a tremendous effort of focus and cooperation. The road map included the current 8086/8088 processors, the highly integrated 80186, then under development, and the next-generation microprocessor featuring memory management, the 80286. Intel even showed 32-bit processors that were in the earliest stages of development. We etched the road maps onto wooden plaques and presented them to our customers. It was a big gamble to show products so far into the future, because it gave our competition a clear target to shoot at. It also put Intel's credibility on the line. Our message was simple: "We have the complete products for you, from chips to development systems to comprehensive support. We have a clear product road map into the future that you can depend on for your new products. We are committed to providing software compatibility of our future microprocessors to protect your investments. We will provide you with leading technology and high quality. Come with us!"

And they did. We waged the Crush campaign with a series of technical seminars for engineers and executive pitches for CEOs and VPs of engineering, marketing, and purchasing. The reaction was truly outstanding. Intel put together a complete products picture, which none of our competitors had done before. After seeing the whole picture, many companies were convinced that choosing Intel microprocessors was indeed the best and safest way to ride into the digital future and tap the broadest product line in the industry.

The Crush campaign succeeded. We exceeded our design win goals. More and more companies were choosing our 16-bit microprocessors. New products based on the 8088 and 8086 became very successful, and customers bought large volumes of our products. This campaign established a yardstick to measure future Intel marketing programs. The marketing task force trained an entire class of marketing people at Intel in the fine art of microprocessor marketing.

In summary, we faced ferocious competition. We started off way behind in the 16-bit race, but admitting that we had a problem was a huge step forward. In the case of the 16-bit microprocessor, we carefully orchestrated the advantages we did have over the competition. We organized a company-wide effort to market our strengths aggressively. We positioned our products clearly and sold our strengths proactively. Our marketing campaign of our complete product offering earned us the lead in the 16-bit market. We became one of a very few companies that succeeded in leading in two successive generations of products. And we went on to win more.

THE BIRTH OF THE PERSONAL COMPUTER

In 1976, Steve Jobs and Steve Wozniak introduced the Apple II computer using our competitor's 6502 microprocessor. The Apple II was an instant success with computer enthusiasts and it was generally labeled the first "personal computer." The Apple II gave birth to an infant personal computer industry almost overnight. The key players were mostly people in their early twenties: Bill Gates of Microsoft, Steve Jobs of Apple, Gary Kildal of Digital Research, and Dan Bricklin of Visicorp, to name just a few.

THE IBM PC IS BORN

IBM, the giant of the computer industry, decided it couldn't stand by and watch a bunch of youngsters lead the new small computer market. In 1979, IBM formed a "tiger team" in Boca Raton, Florida, to come up with a personal computer to compete with Apple. The team was given carte blanche; they were not bound by the usual IBM rules of using internal proprietary technology. Intel's Crush team visited Boca Raton during this time, and the IBM people seemed impressed with our microprocessor pitch. At the time, IBM was buying lots of memory chips from Intel, so Intel was a major supplier and a known entity. The Boca Raton team knew what they needed to do to get into the PC market quickly: pick a commercial microprocessor and a commercial operating system, offer several popular applications such as the Visicalc spreadsheet, and build a low-cost, high-quality microcomputer befitting IBM's image.

The microprocessor would be the linchpin of the whole design. IBM did not particularly want to use the 6502 chip, because Apple was using it. They wanted a 16-bit machine, to leapfrog over Apple's 8-bit. They wanted to build a low-cost computer that could run plenty of software. The Intel 8088 fit the bill perfectly. Intel had just lowered its price. CP/M, Microsoft Basic, and many other software programs ran on the 8088. Intel offered all the necessary support chips to go along with the 8088, making the system hardware design easy. Intel also offered a powerful development system and complete tools to facilitate microcomputer design. Intel provided on-site technical support and assistance to IBM's engineers. And Intel had a strong futures story that included the powerful 80286 and eventually 32-bit products. In short, Intel offered a complete product line, not just devices, and that was what the Boca Raton team wanted. IBM made the monumental decision to use the Intel 8088 microprocessor and started engineering development right away. Although it showed up on Intel's weekly update as just one more design win for 1980, the Boca Raton team's selection of the Intel 8088 was the biggest win ever for Intel. As Bill Davidow later said, "We knew it was an important win. We didn't realize it was the only win."

The IBM PC was introduced in 1981 with a Charlie Chaplin–like figure as its mascot, signifying that this computer was for everyone. Both Microsoft's DOS* and Digital Research's CP/M* were offered as operating systems, along with several applications such as Visicalc. The product was an instant success. All of a sudden, with the IBM name, the personal computer became a legitimate product category.

THE IBM PC-COMPATIBLE BUSINESS EMERGES

Just like Microsoft, which could sell its DOS operating system to anyone, Intel could sell 8088 microprocessors to anyone as well. Many people realized they could build an IBM-compatible PC very easily by buying an Intel 8088 processor, Microsoft DOS, and other commercially available components. IBM actually had a proprietary piece of software in the PC, but several companies reverse-engineered that software and offered it to all comers.

By 1983, the whole new industry of IBM-compatible PCs emerged as a high-volume business. Ben Rosen, a leading semiconductor analyst who had been closely following the semiconductor and PC industries, decided to form a venture capital firm called Sevin & Rosen. His first two investments were Lotus Development Corporation and Compaq Computer Corporation. Lotus developed a much improved spreadsheet called 1-2-3 that tapped the IBM PC's 16-bit power to offer not only spreadsheets but also simple-to-use graphics and database capabilities. Compaq was a company started by Rod Canion and several other Texas Instruments engineers who

---

*These are trademarks of the respective companies.

built a compact PC with improved graphics that was 100 percent compatible with the IBM PC. Both of these products became instant successes and launched two very successful companies. They became leaders of the emerging PC market by being the first movers to take advantage of the power of the new 8088 microprocessor.

IBM moved on quickly to develop the second-generation PC. In 1984, IBM launched the PC-AT, based on Intel's newest processor, the 80286. The IBM PC-AT went on to become the de facto standard PC design for almost ten years. The key technology bases were Microsoft's DOS operating system and Intel's 286 microprocessor. The PC-AT was a low-cost design, yet its capabilities were easily expandable by adding memory, graphics, and networking cards into the system. It was a great PC and became extremely popular. The demand exploded. This stable PC platform was a dream for many new companies eager to build compatible PCs to satisfy the huge demand. In addition to many hardware startups, many software companies were launched to offer new products for this fast-growing PC market. These were the formative years of the huge PC market. As the leader of this emerging market, IBM was the most powerful player and set the direction that others followed.

VOLUME FOLLOWS INDUSTRY STANDARDS

Right from the beginning of the company, Gordon Moore set a simple guideline for Intel: to focus on volume products. A company that builds a custom product for one customer finds its business tied exclusively to that one customer's sales, including all the ups and downs of their products. A company that builds noncustom products that can be sold in volume to many customers will have a much more balanced business that is not unduly affected by one or two companies. More importantly, as explained in Chapter 1, noncustom silicon-technology products can be manufactured in high volumes with associated cost and performance improvements in each new generation. This allows prices to fall as costs go down, which in turn generates bigger demand and higher volumes.

A critical factor in producing high-volume products is to build those products according to industry specifications that are accepted by everyone. In the early days of the VCR, there were two competing standards: Beta and VHS. Both were technically sound, but the existence of two competing video standards was confusing to consumers and bad for retailers, who had to stock both formats. After a few years, VHS won in the marketplace and became the de facto standard, to the benefit of consumers and retailers.

The same process governs most high-technology markets. Whoever gets there first establishes a benchmark against which everyone else is measured. Although there are standard-setting bodies, such as the IEEE in the computer world, these are often too slow at establishing standards. It's difficult to get committee members to agree when they represent companies locked in fierce competition. Intel has always chosen to push volume and let the standards take care of themselves. The more volume you have, the bigger market you represent to others wanting to build compatible products. Very soon, the highest-volume products become de facto standards that everybody follows.

In the case of microprocessors, it was important to establish an architecture (a set of instructions that tells the microprocessor what to do) and processor bus (the communications bridge between the processor and the rest of the chips in the system) that many companies would adopt. Intel was successful in establishing both, starting with the 8080. Microsoft was successful in establishing a standard operating system, MS-DOS, and a programming language, Microsoft Basic, in the emerging PC industry. To this day, Intel microprocessors and Microsoft operating systems remain the pillars of the basic PC platform upon which other companies build PC products. They have provided the stable foundation needed for a high-volume marketplace.

De facto, volume-driven standards are critically important in establishing a new product category. They make it easier for other companies to develop supporting products, and they form a healthy infrastructure for the growth of the whole industry. In the early days, Intel persuaded many independent software and hardware vendors to develop products that worked well with Intel microprocessors. Their products, with ours, provided a complete solutions for customers. They needed us, and we needed them. Once a de facto, volume-based standard is established, everyone benefits—especially customers—because products from different vendors work together and the end result is there are more choices and lower costs for the customers. Therefore, it is important that the industry work together to adopt de facto standards to drive the overall volume up.

The invention of the microprocessor created a new microprocessor industry. We came up with a new business model to offer the complete products, including not only microprocessors but support chips, software tools, development systems, and technical support. Intel also created a new marketing approach that addressed the diverse needs of several decision-makers: the CEO, the system engineer, and the purchasing manager. We developed a long-term product road map that showed our commitment to future. In the process of creating this new industry, we also nurtured and stimulated a new infrastructure that supported new markets for other companies such as independent hardware and software vendors, distribution channels, etc. As a result, Intel, Microsoft, and other early leaders helped generate a wealth of business opportunities for companies wishing to participate in the exciting new PC business. Together we created a whole new industry.

CHAPTER THREE

FOSTER AN INNOVATIVE ENVIRONMENT

ONE OF THE KEYS TO INTEL'S SUCCESS HAS BEEN OUR ABILITY TO generate a steady stream of fresh, new ideas in all areas of the company. This quality is critical to any company working in a fast-paced industry, where today's innovation quickly becomes yesterday's news. How do you create and foster an innovative environment in which breakthrough products are the norm rather than an occasional fluke? How do you encourage employees to think creatively and take risks without gambling the company's resources away?

MMX™ TECHNOLOGY: HOW TO HIT A HOME RUN

In January 1997, Intel introduced an innovative technology for its Pentium processors that helps these chips process multimedia data— sound, graphics, and video—faster and more smoothly. Pentium processors with MMX™ technology achieved instant popularity with consumers. We clearly had hit a home run with this product.

MULTIMEDIA EXCITEMENT

Back in 1992, multimedia was a new, exciting concept in personal computing, and there was a great deal of excitement about bringing great video and sound to PCs. A number of companies were developing software and hardware solutions to make that happen. One of the first to succeed was Creative Labs, which developed a sound card called the SoundBlaster; it soon became widely adopted by the industry. Soon after, a startup company called Media Vision built an add-in kit that included a sound card, a CD-ROM drive, and other elements to convert an ordinary PC into a multimedia PC. Demand was extremely high, and Media Vision did well. A new era of personal computing was clearly upon us.

There were different ways of adding multimedia capability to PCs. And there was clearly a need for multimedia interoperability, as well as a low-cost way to incorporate these capabilities into PCs. The natural place to add this capability was in the microprocessor. Multimedia functions were not much different from other computing functions. As the processor capability increased according to Moore's Law, it would be natural to apply some of that power to accelerate multimedia functions. Intel recognized a market need for pulling multimedia functionality into the microprocessor and set about figuring out the best way to do so.

NURTURE FRAGILE CREATIVE IDEAS

A number of people from different parts of Intel (Santa Clara, Portland, and Haifa) came up with many ideas on how we might incorporate multimedia extensions into the existing Intel microprocessor instruction set. The open environment at Intel encourages people to be critical of our own products and technologies with the hope of stimulating good discussions for improving them. So the debates and discussions about how to implement multimedia raged on for quite some time.

In June of 1993, a strategic discussion meeting was held at which many of Intel's best architects presented their ideas on how to add new instructions to the Pentium processor to accelerate multimedia functions. At the end of the meeting, the team of architects was asked to consolidate the various ideas and prepare a proposal for a single set of instructions and a new product line. A small group under the leadership of two Intel architects, Fred Pollack and Uri Weiser, worked hard to pull the plan together.

Unfortunately, they ran into a lot of resistance. A number of other architects—and several general managers—opposed their plans, because the changes would impact products already in development. There were many different opinions on what instructions to add, what products to incorporate into this new technology, and the timetable. The debate went on for so long that the team driving the technology forward became very frustrated. By late 1993, we had made little progress. But the architecture team pushed ahead with support from the senior managers because one thing was clear: multimedia applications were clearly the hot growth area for the future. If we did not act quickly to implement MMX technology, somebody else would, leaving us in the dust.

As the technical team continued to move forward, it began to make better progress. A number of good ideas surfaced on how to implement the new instructions utilizing the existing floating-point chip area on the Pentium processor. This made the cost of incorporating the new features minimal. The software companies that we talked to were excited about the new instructions set, which would improve the performance of their existing products as well as enable new classes of multimedia applications.

GET THE WHOLE COMPANY BEHIND A SINGLE GOAL

By late 1993, it was clear that the creative stage was coming to a close and it was time to move to the next phase—establishing and implementing a clear business strategy. We embarked on a disciplined process to make MMX technology happen with clear timetables and milestones. We organized a series of meetings culminating at the executive-staff-level Group Strategic Review (GSR) in February 1994. These meetings involved all parts of the company, since it was absolutely essential for everyone in the company to pull in the same direction to make this major technology a success. In order to implement the enhanced instruction set, we had to implement it across the board for all future Intel microprocessors, because software compatibility is critical to Intel's business. In addition, it was necessary to work with all the relevant software developers so they could take advantage of this new technology in a timely manner, another major undertaking. Of course, we had to have a clear idea of how to position our new products and devise a comprehensive marketing program for them.

At the February 1994 GSR, the team made its proposal, and we had intense discussions on the pros and cons of this approach, a good example of our constructive confrontation culture (to be discussed later in more detail). CEO Andy Grove was skeptical and wanted to see the end-user benefits quantified. The team went back and gathered concrete evidence to show Andy how much better multimedia applications would run with this new technology. Andy was delighted with the results and gave us the go-ahead to incorporate MMX technology across the entire microprocessor product line. After working on this for more than two years, the team was elated.

I decided that the first product incorporating the MMX technology would be a Pentium processor to be developed in Haifa, Israel, code-named the P55C. We also decided to start a whole new organization to work with key software application developers to help them develop MMX technology–capable applications and supply them with needed software development tools. In parallel to this, we began developing a major marketing program to promote MMX technology broadly to both OEM (Original Equipment Manufacturers) customers and PC end users. The whole corporation lined up all its resources to make the Pentium processor with MMX technology a great success.

We had a clear, simple goal in mind: to produce processors that would make multimedia software run great. After the GSR, we took a very disciplined approach to ensure that we executed really well on all the programs, from chip design to application software development to the marketing campaign. We held comprehensive program reviews on a monthly basis throughout 1994 and 1995 and weekly through 1996, when we were one year away from introducing the product. It was one of the most ambitious programs that we have ever undertaken.

The first step in inventing a brand-new product is a sharp focus on the end result. The whole MMX technology development effort started out with a clear and urgent need in mind: how to make emerging multimedia applications run great on Intel microprocessors. Some of our brightest people offered a variety of ideas on how to accomplish this. We took all of these ideas and funneled them into a disciplined process by which all the creative juices resulted in a single MMX instruction set architecture.

Solid and detailed planning came next. We planned the product line, the software, and the marketing programs in 1994, two full years before the product was introduced. All this took a substantial amount of time, but the long discussions and debates during the early phases flushed out most of the critical issues and allowed the whole company to align its resources to achieve the common goal.

The next step was to develop the products: the microprocessors with MMX technology and the associated software. It was risky asking the Israel design team to design a high-volume microprocessor chip. Their prior experience had been developing several successful, but low-volume, communication and co-processor chips. They had to learn quickly about the key issues in designing a fast-ramping, volume product from other people in the company. And they did. It was also taking a risk to insert this brand-new technology into an existing Pentium processor. But the team was ready for the challenge and gladly took on this big assignment.

However, by early 1995 the design team ran into severe difficulties coping with the technical complexity of the chip, and the schedule had to be pushed out. We had to marshal all our resources to resolve this crisis. A task force of people from Santa Clara, Phoenix, Portland, and Haifa worked day and night to turn the situation around. This was the crucial juncture for the project. Either the team pulled itself together and moved forward, or the project might well falter and never recover. I spent a great deal of time coaching team members in overcoming and solving many tough issues.

I went to Israel in May 1995 for a detailed program review and was delighted to see that the situation had improved dramatically and that the team's momentum and confidence were returning. This team had heard about the "bet" I made with another design team[10] just a few months earlier, and they proposed a similarly aggressive "bet." They bet me that they could hit key milestones on schedule, such as the first demo (slated for December 1995), performance metrics, quality, and cost. If they won, I would send them on an exotic vacation. If they lost, they would wash my car. I gladly accepted the bet, and the team returned to their work with renewed enthusiasm.

They worked intensively for eight months and produced the first working silicon by December 1995, exactly when they had said they would. I was asked to go to the lab in Santa Clara to see a demonstration of the first working Pentium processor with MMX technology running a number of multimedia applications. They ran beautifully. It was an incredible high to see these wonderful people produce such great results. Everybody was laughing and cheering at

FIGURE 5   PENTIUM PROCESSOR WITH MMX TECHNOLOGY

Source: Intel

achieving this major milestone. We shipped the first ten systems to Microsoft and other developers to get software development going by January 1996, exactly as we had said we would. Many of the software developers were astounded at how well the chip worked the first time out. We were on our way!!

In March 1996, we demonstrated the Pentium processor with MMX technology at a big software industry event, Intermedia, in San Francisco, for the purpose of getting the software community excited about this new technology. We needed all of them to devote development resources to building multimedia applications that would take advantage of MMX technology. We not only demonstrated how well the chips worked to accelerate multimedia applications but also produced strong endorsements from key executives at Microsoft, Macromedia, Adobe, and other leading software developers. These people spoke convincingly about how MMX technology gave a big performance boost to their multimedia software. They were glad to share their positive experience with the conference audience. It was a win-win technology: good for Intel, good for software developers and, most important of all, good for consumers.

As a result of this successful showing at Intermedia, many more software developers started major MMX technology application development. When the Pentium processor with MMX technology was finally introduced on January 8, 1997, more than 20 applications for MMX technology were already on the market. Members of the press and market analysts were thrilled by what they saw and gave the technology phenomenal coverage. Our OEM customers had been working closely with us to develop PC products that incorporated Pentium processors with MMX technology, and they launched a host of new products simultaneous to our worldwide launch. Many of the engineers who developed the chips and software were present at the launch and were elated to see their creations hit the market with such a great reception.

Almost immediately, the buzz was out: MMX technology was

hot! Our marketing organization worked with our ad agency to come up with a number of creative print and TV advertisements targeted at end users. The basic idea was that MMX technology created "fun" for end users. In two of the TV ads, workers wearing bunny suits in an Intel factory suddenly turned into colors and started dancing to pulsating rock music as they put "fun" into Pentium processors with MMX technology. Four TV ads were aired during the Super Bowl on January 26, 1997, and were instant hits. All this great press coverage and memorable advertising created a massive interest in consumers, who went to the stores in huge numbers and bought PCs with Pentium with MMX technology inside. Within 30 days of the launch, about 40 percent of retail computer sales were for PCs with Pentium processors with MMX technology. I remember talking to one of my attorney friends during this time, who said, "I heard that the Pentium with MMX technology is great. I'm going to buy a notebook computer with it."

We had just hit a home run! To top it all off, the Cannes Film Festival awarded its first digital technology award to Andy Grove for Intel's MMX technology. The award acknowledged Andy's contribution to creating new technologies that benefited the film industry. Andy accepted the award on May 16, 1997, in Santa Clara, California, via an Internet video phone call with Cannes, France, using the very technology the award celebrated. How appropriate!

KEY VALUES THAT ENCOURAGE INNOVATION

The MMX technology story is an example of how innovative ideas make it from the drawing board at Intel to the consumer's home. The key to Intel's knack for generating innovation is rooted in Intel's well-defined corporate culture. Six key pillars to Intel's culture have been developed and refined over the years:

- Results orientation
- Risk-taking
- Discipline

- Quality
- Customer orientation
- Great place to work

The first three are critical to creating an innovative environment and will be discussed here. The last three, along with more details on results orientation, will be described in Chapter 7.

FOCUS ON RESULTS

Results orientation means that we focus on delivering measurable results on time, as promised. Andy Grove drives himself and the whole organization to achieve concrete results. In his book, *High Output Management*,[11] Andy shares his ideas on how to get exceptional results from an organization.

We believe that our focus on results motivates everyone to come up with creative ideas and turn them into something concrete—a product, process, or service—that delivers value for our customers. Often, innovation comes about because we have to achieve certain key results. In the case of MMX technology, we were driven by the strong desire to produce high-volume, low-cost solutions to improve multimedia computing for our customers. In the case of the first microprocessor, the 4004, we were driven by the need to come up with an innovative solution not only for one customer, Busicom, but also so that Intel would have a volume product for many customers. In both these cases and others, innovative ideas sprang up to help us achieve the desired results.

REWARD RISK-TAKING

The second pillar of Intel's culture is risk-taking. What I am talking about is informed risk, where one clearly understands the downside risks and upside rewards. No one is advocating blindly jumping into any risky situation. But we are advocating taking informed risks after thoroughly examining the possible options and alternatives. Innovation cannot happen without informed risk-taking. Innovating *means* trying something new. It is certain that some new approaches will not work. In an environment that encourages risk-taking, failure has to be OK. Failures often lead to success. This is how innovation comes about: try, experiment, fail, and succeed.

Starting a new company is risk-taking of the first order. Both Robert Noyce and Gordon Moore did this twice, in starting Fairchild and Intel. They became role models and made risk-taking a major element of the Intel culture. Noyce was a gracious man with a fascination for the future. One of his more famous sayings was, "Don't be encumbered by history—go off and do something wonderful." When he talked about new ideas his eyes would sparkle like a child's. He loved new ideas and constantly encouraged people to explore them. His favorite saying was, "Don't worry, just do it!" This had a magical effect on people. Gordon Moore always says, "Change is our ally." He constantly encourages managers at Intel to initiate or take advantage of change. With Bob and Gordon's encouragement, it was easy to take risks and experiment with new ways of doing things.

In addition, to proactively encourage risk-taking, it is necessary to accept the consequences of failure. At Intel, it is OK to fail when one takes an informed risk. A good example was Intel's venture into the electronic watch business in the mid-1970s. Intel found itself a major supplier of inexpensive digital circuits that formed the basis of electronic watches. So the company decided to enter the consumer electronic watch business with a venture called Microma. It turned out that, while Intel knew a lot about integrated circuits, it knew little about the fashion and consumer business. The Microma business failed. However, this informed risk was based on our observation that electronic movements in watches were replacing mechanical movements and we might be able to play a major role in this technology transition. A number of Intel people were recruited into Microma, but none of their careers suffered when it failed. All moved on to other jobs at Intel. In such an environment, people are not afraid to take informed risks.

For stories with happier endings, risk-taking was what got Intel into the memory business, the microprocessor business, and the communications business. In essence, risk-taking is at the heart of high technology. Many high-tech companies have taken informed risks and become very successful in the process. Apple took a risk by building a small computer for individual computer enthusiasts but few other obvious customers. Netscape took a risk by offering a Web browser to exploit the infant World Wide Web. Many Intel senior managers do a good job of role-modeling risk-taking. Gordon Moore pushed for getting Intel into the unknown semiconductor memory business when core memory was the mainstream in 1968. He also encouraged Ted Hoff and Frederico Faggin in 1969 to build the first microprocessors with no clear ideas on how they would be used. Andy Grove made the risky decision to pull Intel out of the memory business in 1985 and focus the company on the uncertain microprocessor business. Andy took another risk in launching the "Intel Inside" campaign to build Intel's brand recognition. More recently, he also pushed Intel into the communications business as a necessary step to making the PC the universal device for communications. I was one of a number of managers who took a risk with the MMX technology. The examples go on.

DEMAND DISCIPLINE

The third pillar of Intel culture is discipline. For years, Intel had an infamous 8:00 A.M. sign-in; if you arrived more than five minutes later, you had to sign in. The idea was to impress upon everyone that everything at Intel started at 8:00 A.M., including meetings and phone calls. Because we work in such a team-oriented and geographically spread out environment, we all depend on one another being at our desks at expected times. If you're not there or don't show up at meetings on time, those who are waiting for you are wasting their time. The 8:00 A.M. sign-in was a symbol that we needed discipline in everything we did. We eliminated the sign-in during the late

1980s when we felt that the organization was doing well in the area of discipline.

Perhaps the best example of discipline in a large organization is the military. One starts the day on time, and keeps one's quarters orderly and one's weapon clean at all times. In fact, new soldiers are typically trained in discipline before they are trained in anything else. The reasoning is simple: to succeed in battle, the army must be disciplined in everything it does. The business world demands similar discipline in order to be competitive and successful.

Another symbol of discipline at Intel is our "Mr. Clean" inspections. These are conducted monthly by senior managers, who inspect every one of our facilities and score each area for cleanliness and orderliness. Areas receiving poor scores must be cleaned up quickly. Again, the idea is that we must have safe, uncluttered work areas to carry out quality work, whether we are in manufacturing, engineering, marketing, or finance. While the 8:00 A.M. sign-in and Mr. Clean inspections are largely symbolic, Intel works hard to instill the value of discipline in all aspects of its operation. Discipline is absolutely necessary for our success. We can't develop products and move them into manufacturing if the engineering and marketing organizations are sloppy and do not meet their commitments. In order to transform innovative ideas to results, one must have a disciplined and organized approach to make things happen on time.

When I was working at Fairchild, there was little evidence of discipline or results orientation. Engineering groups came up with lots of good ideas but with no clear end result in mind. The marketing team was very creative but sloppy in meeting its commitments. As a result, it was incredibly difficult to bring new products to market, as all parts of the organization were not moving with precision and synchronization toward the same goal. This was squarely due to the lack of discipline and a clear focus on results.

Starting in the 1970s, one way we got everyone marching together at Intel was to call GYAT (get your act together) meetings. Representatives from engineering, marketing, manufacturing, and finance came together once a week to present their schedules, status, and interdependencies. It was amazing how well these diverse groups marched to the same rigorous schedule once they bought into a common goal and understood what everyone else was doing.

In the case of MMX technology, the tasks were big and complex. Without a sharp focus on end results and a relentlessly disciplined approach to making things happen, the technology might never have become reality. We held monthly and eventually weekly review meetings with all groups to make sure everything was in synchronization and any problems that surfaced were solved quickly. Making innovation happen is very hard work.

CREATE AN OPEN ENVIRONMENT FOR IDEAS

To create an environment that is conducive to innovation, risk-taking must be an accepted value, people must drive to produce results, and everyone needs to conduct business in a disciplined manner. There are other important ingredients: senior managers must act as role models in encouraging innovation. The work environment must be open for free discussions on new ideas as well as problems.

Successful high-technology companies thrive on the free flow of information. This ebb and flow of new ideas is often chaotic and messy, but it's the only way to ensure that new ideas will surface and multiply. Conversely, you can't invent great ideas where there is no forum to think, explore, and exchange. We have found that ideas get better with lots of intense interactive discussion and debate. When two or three engineers thoroughly debate and explore an idea, the end result is usually much better than if one person thinks about it alone. An innovative engineering idea is usually not good enough. It is the interaction of customers, marketers, and engineers that typically generates the sparks for great products.

The invention of the microprocessor at Intel was instigated by such a flurry of sparks: a customer request, a lot of discussion and speculation, then a bold act of risk-taking. Gordon Moore encouraged the team to develop this new device later known as a microprocessor, even though no one knew what good it would do. The attitude was, "Gee, this may open a whole new market for us," and indeed it did. Faggin and his team were extremely disciplined in their design efforts, and they had clear results in mind. There was innovation at every step of the development from initial architecture to chip design to manufacturing to marketing. The team was results-oriented and practiced discipline all the way.

We have found that innovation must happen at the grass-roots level and the ideas must then be exploited quickly. First-line managers must encourage innovation from their teams. One clever idea that our Portland Microprocessor Division implemented was a "Skunk Works Award." People who come up with great ideas are given the "Skunk Works Award" on the spot. It's a great way to visibly encourage innovation at every level of the company.

As Intel gets bigger, encouraging innovative ideas to surface and incorporating them into products gets harder. In 1992, I discussed this problem with several people at Intel, and we came up with the idea of an Innovators Day to encourage employees to bring forth new and creative ideas. We would award $100,000 to the winners and allow them to explore their ideas full time for a year. We hoped that some of these ideas would become winning products or tools.

On our first Innovators Day in 1993 we received more than 100 submissions. We selected ten finalists, who presented their ideas to a panel of judges consisting of Gordon Moore, John Crawford, Les Vadasz, Fred Pollack, and myself, in an open meeting that was attended by anyone who was interested. The quality of the ideas was impressive. We debated for a long time and ended up awarding two winners. One candidate proposed novel ideas on how to make the cache memory run much faster. Another proposed using 3D displays for computer-aided design tools in our chip design.

All the finalists shared their ideas in an open poster session attended by many Intel employees. Lots of new ideas were generated by free discussions in this open environment. One winner's idea was eventually implemented in new Intel products. We were very pleased with the results, as we had expected something like a 10 to 20 percent success rate, and the 50 percent success rate really surprised us.

We held our second and third Innovators Days in 1995 and 1997. The number of submissions increased to 160 and 230, respectively, and we awarded four and five winners for these successive years. One 1995 winner saw his proposed idea implemented in the Pentium processor with MMX technology. That feature in the chip helped the engineers to shorten the time to market the chip and to improve the speed of the chip by a factor of two. As a result, we were able to achieve greater chip performance in about half the time that the previous generation took. A great result indeed!

Innovators Day provides one more avenue for innovative ideas to surface and gain wide visibility within the company. Senior managers encourage risk-taking by awarding funding for new ideas. They also spend time with the innovators to listen to and discuss their ideas. Lastly, the event provides a forum for several hundred people to gather and discuss new ideas, stimulating a flow of creative juices that continues beyond Innovators Day.

ENCOURAGE INNOVATION IN ALL AREAS

We encourage innovation not only in product and technology areas but throughout our operation. One example of novel innovation occurred in the treasury department in the early 1990s, then run by Harold Hughes (now chairman of Pandesic, a joint venture with SAP to market electronic commerce products). The treasury manages the corporate cash to earn the highest possible interest rate without taking on unnecessary risks. The basic concept is to move money wherever the interest rate is highest. Most companies hire Wall Street money managers to handle this complex task. Harold looked at these firms and discovered that they located the highest interest rate by phone, which was a slow and tedious process. Some companies were just beginning to use computers, but they used older computers with poor performance.

Harold said, "We can do better." He proposed the use of the fastest Pentium processor–based PC available to tap directly into the worldwide money network. By using high-speed PCs, he could find the highest interest rate in the world before other traders. Gordon gave Harold his blessing, and he was off and running. The plan worked, and in short order our treasury department was beating the Wall Street shops by earning the highest interest rates in the business. Risk-taking? Yes. Results orientation? Yes. Discipline? Yes. Role-modeling by senior managers? Yes, yes!

A great marketing innovation was Dennis Carter's push to create consumer brand awareness for Intel, which had been known until then only within the technical community as a semiconductor company. As Andy Grove's technical assistant, Dennis had pioneered a very successful print advertising campaign in the 1980s urging users of 286-based PCs to move to 386 processor–based PCs. Dennis felt strongly that establishing the Intel brand in consumers' minds would bring us long-lasting value. He argued convincingly that a well-established brand such as Coke, Disney, or Sony lasts for years, while technological advantages come and go. Andy agreed and made consumer awareness of Intel the next major strategic move for the company. The result was the "Intel Inside" campaign, started in 1991. Andy and Dennis drove the "Intel Inside" campaign to establish Intel's name in everyone's mind and to heighten the importance of the microprocessor inside the computer. This was a major innovation. Dennis and his team executed the program with clear end results in mind (to make people prefer Intel processors) and with exceptional discipline and rigor. The "Intel Inside" campaign made Intel a household word around the world in a few years and created strong user preference for an Intel processor inside the computer. Today, the "Intel Inside" label on the PC represents technology and quality to end users; they know they're buying the most advanced technology, as well as the highest-quality products. This campaign was a good example of risk-taking, as few "ingredient" products have been successfully branded, and no semiconductor company had ever succeeded in building consumer brand awareness. It was results-oriented, as Andy and Dennis set out to build equity in the Intel brand, then made it happen. It required discipline in execution of the marketing programs.

How do you foster an innovative environment that allows you to invent great products time after time? First, you have to instill a fanatical focus on results. Effort alone is not enough. Concrete results count. Second, you must encourage and nurture informed risk-taking, while recognizing that failure is OK. Third, you must ensure that teams take a disciplined approach to turning great ideas into great products. The combination of these three values—results orientation, risk-taking, and discipline—is essential to allowing innovative ideas to surface and then turning them into great products. Senior managers must role-model these values and nurture fragile new ideas through periods of intense scrutiny and questioning. You must foster an open environment in which ideas and problems can be freely argued and debated. Most important, you must expect excellence and never cease asking, "How can we do better?"

CHAPTER FOUR

DELIVER A COMPELLING PRODUCT ROAD MAP

AT THE HEART OF EVERY SUCCESSFUL HIGH-TECHNOLOGY COMPANY today is a compelling product line that delights customers. It is relatively easy to create one great product. It is also easy to keep extending a successful product line in a linear fashion. However, Intel works hard to offer a compelling product road map that serves an ever expanding and dynamic marketplace over many years. While we have often succeeded, we have also stumbled at times. But we've learned from our mistakes and moved on to build better and better products that exceed our customers' expectations over and over again. This chapter describes our efforts to build and expand our product road map.

GOOD, BETTER, BEST

According to Alfred Sloan Jr. in *My Years with General Motors*,[12] one of the key elements of GM's success in overtaking Ford was its ability to offer a complete product line that covered the whole spectrum of automotive needs, from the economical Chevrolet to the mid-range Pontiac, Oldsmobile, and Buick, and to the high-end Cadillac. In addition, GM made consistent yearly model changes to keep the product line fresh and to persuade buyers to upgrade their cars as their incomes rose. In contrast, Ford started out with only one model and one color, and the rest is history. Since then, most consumer products companies have offered products in the "good, better, best" segments to attract different buyers. The danger, however, is that the segmentation can become too complex and confusing.

For Intel's memory business, we basically offered one memory size at a time. For example, our first popular semiconductor memory was the 1103 with 1K bits. As 4K became available, it quickly replaced 1K. Today, the dominant memory size is 64M (64 million); the next one will be 254M.

When we offered the 386 microprocessor line, we had only two products: the 386 SX with a 16-bit bus and the 386 DX with a 32-bit bus (see more details in Chapter 8, "Make the Right Strategic Transitions"). Beginning with the 486 processor family, we began to think about expanding our offerings to enable OEM customers to offer a "good, better, best" lineup to end users. We eventually came up with three offerings: the 486 SX without a floating-point unit, the 486 DX with a floating-point unit, and the 486 DX2 with "clock doubler" technology (described in Chapter 9). This strategy worked very well, as it was exactly what end users wanted in terms of a full range of choices. It also gave our OEM customers (and Intel) a great deal of pricing flexibility. We priced the SX low for high-volume, entry-level products; we priced the DX higher for the mid-range; and we put a premium price on the DX2 because of its high-performance capability. OEMs followed the same strategy. They offered a full line of "good, better, best" products, giving end users a full spectrum of products from which to choose. It was a win-win for all parties. This was the beginning of our product road map.

MICROPROCESSOR ROAD MAP: GUIDE TO THE FUTURE OF COMPUTING

Despite the automotive analogy, there are several major differences between microprocessors (and other high-technology products) and automobiles. For automobiles, market segments stay basically the same over time. The Cadillac remains the top of the line for GM, and Chevrolet remains at the volume economy end (though the Saturn was later added below Chevrolet). The auto industry talks only about today's lineup and seldom discusses future product plans. These are all characteristic of a more mature industry where there is little fundamental product innovation and improvement.

For high-technology products, the situation is dramatically different. Moore's Law predicts that capability and performance will double every 18 to 24 months. As a result, our product road map shows significant performance and feature improvements over time.

In the 486 processor family, an operating speed of 66 MHz was tops at the end of 1992 but quickly slid to a mid-range position by early 1993 when it was replaced by the 100-MHz part. Just a year later, the Intel Pentium processor took the top position, while the 66-MHz 486 DX2 went to the bottom. In the automotive world, this same pace of innovation would result in the Cadillac moving to the Chevrolet range in two years and being replaced by cars with 12-cylinder engines that got 60 miles to the gallon a year later!

Intel put together a microprocessor road map in the late 1970s as part of our Crush marketing campaign to show our customers that we had clear plans for the next two product generations. This early road map was presented at a very high level with major product features, giving the general direction of our future products for long-term planning purposes. By 1991, our internal road map had become a lot more specific, with detailed product speeds and expected volumes by quarter, over an 18-month period, the limit of our visibility. We first used this document to help us in planning our new products. We shared this road map with a few key PC manufacturers that participated in our product planning process. They found it extremely useful in planning their own products. We spent a great deal of time discussing with customers when and where we should introduce specific products, and they usually offered good suggestions. In fact, we often changed the road map based on their inputs. The road map discussions have always been very interactive and productive.

As time went on, we evolved this process to where we now put together a draft of our road map and review it with a few key customers. They provide detailed feedback, which helps us to finalize the plan. Then, we communicate the road map to all of our customers on a quarterly basis. Intel's product road maps have become significant industry events, and our customers use them in planning their own products.

An example of our product road map for 1997 is shown in Figure 6. There are several points worth noting. First, we segment the PC market by price points from the high end through mid-range to low-end products. These segments are distinguished not only by the different processors but also by memory size, hard disk size, CD-ROM capability, multimedia capability, and so on.

Second, a processor of a given speed (MHz) moves rapidly from the high end to the low end in about a year. What that means to the end users is that, for the same price, PC performance goes up by about 50 percent a year (this is an average—sometimes it is faster and sometimes slower). Looking at it differently, one can buy a low-end product today that wore a high-end price tag just a year ago. This is Moore's Law in action for end users. PC capabilities keep advancing at a rapid rate, enabling consumers to buy very powerful PCs at very low prices. This, in turn, attracts more PC users, which expands the entire high-technology market.

Third, the road map shows the introduction of a brand-new generation of products with MMX technology in the first quarter of 1997, which started at the high end but moved rapidly to lower segments with increasing volume. This product road map basically outlines Intel's microprocessor offerings for the whole PC industry over the course of the year.

Over time, Intel road maps have become strategic documents that not only cover our total microprocessor offering, but also show where we are putting emphasis and how quickly we're ramping new products into production. It also shows which products will soon be obsolete and taken off the road map. These road maps put a lot of re-

FIGURE 6   INTEL'S 1997 PRODUCT ROAD MAP

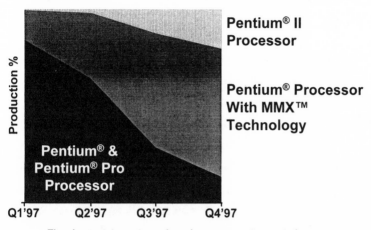

The above statements are based upon current expectations.
These statements are forward looking and actual results may differ

Source: Intel

sponsibility on us. They indicate what we will deliver, and we'd better do it, because others depend on us for their future programs. We
also took on the responsibility of having a complete product line that
our customers can depend on to build their own complete offerings.
In the days of the 386 processors, we had only two products, which
was insufficient for our customers. Around 1993, we adopted a "no
holes" strategy in which we developed products for every price point
on our road map. Our customers could look to Intel in developing
their own complete product lines. The no-holes strategy has been
very successful and continues today. In 1997, we saw a strong market
demand for low-cost PCs. We responded quickly by charting a team
to target products for that segment.

EXPAND FROM MICROPROCESSORS TO CHIP SETS

When IBM adopted our 8088 microprocessor for its first PC, they also
adopted all our support chips necessary to build a PC motherboard.[13]

During the 286 time frame in the early 1980s, when we were devoting all our resources to developing microprocessors, we did not develop new support chips to go with our microprocessors. Several companies promptly jumped on this opportunity to fill the product vacuum left behind.

One of them, Chips and Technologies, integrated many of these support chips into a low-cost chip set that was fully compatible with the IBM PC. They successfully sold their chip set to PC clone makers. Taking a leaf from our philosophy to offer "complete products," they supplied the clone makers with a prototype motherboard. This was a significant step forward for the PC industry. The availability of a compatible chip set, with only a few chips together with a completed designed motherboard, made it extremely easy for anyone to build a PC motherboard. You simply bought the chip set, built a motherboard based on the prototype, put in an Intel processor, added memory and a hard disk, loaded Microsoft MS-DOS, and you were done! This was one of the many reasons why the PC market took off so quickly, as many new companies started up to jump on this opportunity to build lots of PCs.

The downside of this cookie-cutter approach was that the PC architecture was frozen at the IBM PC-AT generation. One of the biggest problems with this design was that the speed of the ISA (Industry Standard Architecture) bus was very slow. As a result, anything that was connected to the bus—hard disk, graphics, and so on—ran very slowly. As time went on, several attempts were made to improve this bus. In the mid-1980s, IBM proposed a bus called MCA (Micro Channel Architecture) to improve the performance of its PS/2 PC line. To counteract that, Compaq Computer proposed another one called EISA (Extended ISA). A battle of the buses—EISA versus MCA—ensued between IBM and Compaq. There were stories each week in the trade press about which side appeared to be winning. Actually, nobody much cared, as neither bus really offered discernible PC performance improvements. Because of the confusion, most manufacturers stayed with the cheaper ISA bus. As a result, the PC industry was stuck with a slow bus for years.

By 1990, I formed a group to look into improving overall PC system performance, with particular emphasis on how to improve the graphics and bus performance. The team investigated many different system architectures and configurations. They built a prototype system to demonstrate a novel bus configuration and saw big improvements in the graphics performance. A number of engineers from Portland and Folsom jumped on this new discovery and designed a new bus architecture that increased the bus speed by a factor of four to five. Their very fine design provided fast links not only to the graphics controller but also to the hard disk and other devices. In addition, by putting several of these high-speed bus channels together, you could create very high-performance input/output for server-class computers. The team had just created an inexpensive new bus that could be used for PCs all the way from low-end desktop to the very high-end servers. We were all very excited with what the team had invented.

This new bus, called PCI (Peripheral Component Interface), offered a quantum jump in PC performance for the first time since the invention of the PC-AT in 1984! In an industry technology forum that we held in 1991, there was tremendous interest from all the participants in how to improve the old ISA bus. One Intel speaker presented the PCI idea and it was enthusiastically received. Many companies wanted to work with us to make the new technology happen. In the interest of advancing the PC architecture, we decided to make PCI an open industry specification and offered to license the PCI specification to all interested parties free of royalties. Seeing this as a good business opportunity, many silicon chip companies started aggressively developing chip sets, graphics controllers, and other products based on PCI. The stage was set to make PCI a commercial reality.

The PCI bus not only promised to boost PC performance in general, it also presented a good business opportunity for our chip set operation in Folsom. Ron Smith, general manager of the unit, became a strong champion of PCI chip sets and renamed his unit the PCI division. However, we ran into lots of resistance in putting resources in this area, because for many years we had poured resources into different chip sets with little return. Several of us (Paul Otellini, Ron Smith, and I, among others) persisted and were able to find some resources to design the first PCI chip set for the 486 processor to test-market the concept. Ron moved rapidly to design that chip set—called Saturn—and demonstrated a fully functioning PC system by Fall Comdex (the major trade show for computer dealers) in November 1992. At this show, we demonstrated the clearly superior graphics performance of the PCI chip set over the older ISA. Our customers saw the benefits and aggressively embraced the PCI product. At about the same time, a group of companies developed a competing bus called VL. So, the bus war erupted again, but this time it was PCI versus VL, with each side touting its virtues. In fact, many 486-based systems used the VL bus.

We focused all our PCI chip set development on the upcoming Pentium processor, as the two really worked well together. The combination of the PCI chip set and the Pentium processor gave PC users exactly what they wanted: a great multimedia PC to run all the new and exciting CD-ROM-based applications. In 1993, we introduced our PCI chip set together with the Pentium processor. Remember, we wanted to offer the complete products to make the job of building PCs easy for our customers. The two products were received with great enthusiasm by the PC industry. The new PC platform combining the Pentium processor and PCI chip set represented a giant step forward in multimedia performance over 486-based PCs. All the leading OEMs jumped on the opportunity to lead with this new platform. Pentium processor–based PCs built with non-PCI chip sets were just not competitive anymore. Both the Pentium processor and the PCI took off in volume at about the same time. All of a sudden, we went from nowhere in the chip set business to shipping four million PCI chip set units in 1994, 20 million units in 1995, and close to 70 million units in 1996. Within a few short years, Intel became the world's leading supplier in the PC chip set market segment.

I vividly remember the big celebration we held for shipping our one-millionth chip set, in Folsom in the spring of 1994. It was an incredible high for everybody in the division—they had worked hard over many years and succeeded in delivering a great product. Since 1993, we have included chip sets in our product road maps with our microprocessors. We have been designing the processors and chip sets together ever since so we can create balanced systems with optimal performance and cost.

EXTEND MICROPROCESSORS TO MOBILE COMPUTERS

The first PCs were all desktop models. Compaq actually invented a new form-factor by introducing a one-piece PC light enough to carry around. Several companies improved on that first design and introduced even smaller and lighter computers that operated on batteries. These mobile PCs opened up a new market which has been growing more rapidly than that of the desktop PC. In 1988, we formed a Mobile and Handheld Products Group to focus on serving the needs of mobile computing. By 1997, the mobile market had grown to about one-fourth of the total PC market.

People usually use notebook computers when they travel or take work home. However, mobile computers are also used in companies where office space is at a premium. The three big requirements for mobile computers are small size, light weight, and low power consumption (for battery operation). We decided to focus on providing microprocessors in special packages that would fit the small form-factor of notebook computers. We also developed special features for these processors to reduce power consumption, aiming to prolong battery life.

Several people within the mobile computing group came up with the idea in the late 1980s that the ideal microprocessor for the mobile market would be a highly integrated, single-chip processor that combined many functions of the support chips like keyboard, liquid crystal display, and disk controllers. Instead of having ten or more components, wouldn't it be nice to have only one—a one-chip computer? This was such a compelling idea that we had already tried it twice before, without much success.

We made the first attempt at a one-chip computer in the early 1980s, when Masatoshi Shima, one of the original designers of the 4004, 8008, and 8080 microprocessors, tried to build a one-chip computer, code-named the PO, at our Japan Design Center. That project failed, because both the complexity and the size of the chip grew too large. The second attempt, started soon after the PO, was the 80186, a less ambitious but still highly integrated version of the 8086 processor that included several support chips right on the main processor. That chip was successful, but not in the PC market, simply because the support chips that were integrated were not exactly the same ones used in the original IBM PC. Because 100 percent PC compatibility was paramount, the 186 could not be used in PCs. The 186 found a successful role in the embedded market for many digital control functions. Despite these setbacks, the idea of developing a one-chip processor for the mobile computer market was really appealing, as it could potentially solve both the size and power problems by reducing the number of chips to one.

The design team set out to design the first integrated processor for the mobile market: the 386 SL. It added a number of support chip functions, as well as power-saving features, to the 386 processor. However, the 386 SL had a lukewarm reception from our customers for several reasons. First, because of the additional engineering work required, the 386 SL came to market approximately two years after its desktop counterpart. Second, its performance fell far short of the desktop versions because of the added complexity on the chip with the integrated support functions. Customers wanted their notebook computers' performance to be nearly equal to that of their desktop computers. Unfortunately, the 386 SL did not meet that expectation. In addition, to take advantage of the extra power-saving features, our OEM customers had to design another board just for the SL. They had to devote more engineering resources to do an additional PC design and they were not willing to do that. As a result, the 386 SL was not well accepted in the marketplace.

We tried one more time with another high-integration part for the mobile market, the 486 SL, and did a better job of getting it out sooner with better performance. But the same problems remained. Simply put, a high-integration mobile part did not offer enough benefits over a non-high-integration part—which came out sooner and could be designed with the latest chip sets—to produce a better-performing, more competitive notebook computer.

We finally realized, after several years on the high-integration path, that the best way to meet the mobile computing requirement for lower power and a smaller footprint was to focus on adding the power-saving features of our high-volume processors so they could fit in a mobile platform. In addition, we would put the chips in small and light packages to fit into small footprints for mobile computing. Beginning with the Pentium processor, we focused on achieving low power and a small package for the mobile market. With this new direction, we were able to offer mobile processors and chip sets that delight our OEM customers. Now we have an excellent mobile-product road map with ever-improving performance and features. By 1996, most notebook computers on the market used low-power Pentium processors.

We learned a lot about what it takes to create compelling microprocessors for different market segments, such as the mobile market. It is important to keep market requirements firmly in mind and not be lulled into a fixed-technology direction, like the high-integration idea, that ends up having more pitfalls than benefits.

ADD SERVER AND WORKSTATION PRODUCTS

A server is a computer that provides shared applications to a number of desktop PCs that are networked together. Servers are very important for several reasons. A combination of powerful servers networked with a number of clients or desktop PCs has emerged as the preferred way of doing business computing, replacing the older minicomputers and mainframes, due to lower cost and more flexibility. In this "client-server" model, powerful applications, such as a database, reside on the server, which is shared by many clients. Clients will have their own local applications, such as word processing, presentation graphics, spreadsheets, and so on. The users have the best of both worlds: local applications to suit one's personal needs and shared applications and data that need to be centralized. As the Internet becomes more pervasive, powerful servers become the heart of information storage and communications. Therefore the server market has been one of the fastest growing segments of computing.

By the late 1980s, most servers were either minicomputers or RISC-based processors (more about RISC-based processors in Chapter 9). Around 1990, Compaq introduced the first PC servers using Intel's 486 and became the first mover in this fast-growing market. Others soon followed Compaq's lead. The PC server market grew rapidly, as they offered far superior price/performance over either minicomputers or RISC-based products.

Servers require high-speed communications between the microprocessor and the memory to handle large numbers of transactions demanded by the many clients. This need is different from that of desktop computers. Craig Kinnie, head of the Intel Architecture Lab, came up with a great idea to improve the server performance

*Trademark

based on the 486. He proposed that we build a super-fast cache memory and connect that directly to the processor bus. The combination would offer much faster transaction processing capability than the stand-alone 486. This was an excellent way to expand our microprocessor product line from desktops to server applications. We launched a project to build this fast cache memory to connect directly with our 50-MHz 486 processors. Getting the cache memory and the 486 processor to work together at 50-MHz was a tough design challenge in 1991. After overcoming many technical difficulties, we succeeded in making the chips work well together (see Chapter 9 for more details) and introduced the 50-MHz parts. Our customers were delighted with this new offering, as it enabled them to build much more powerful servers for this emerging market. Compaq was the first to introduce PC servers based on 486 processors and the fast cache. Their product was an instant success because of its superior price and performance. Compaq has been the leader of the PC server market ever since. Many PC companies soon followed Compaq's lead and entered this market.

Soon after, many server customers told us that multiprocessing capability was really important to expand PC server performance further. They wanted to build servers with multiple processors in them—anywhere from one to four—to offer scalable performance. For example, they could ship a two-processor system with only one processor and an empty socket. Customers could later upgrade these systems by plugging in another processor to gain more performance. We thought that was a great idea. We responded quickly by adding special multiprocessing features to the Pentium processor, cache memory, and the chip set. These chips enabled PC companies to build even more powerful and scalable servers for their customers. As a result of their superior price/performance and scalability, Pentium processor–based servers became very successful in expanding the overall market. We moved on to improve the server performance even more with our Pentium Pro and Pentium II processor product line, discussed later in Chapter 10.

Realizing the importance of this market, Intel formed an Enterprise Server Group in 1994, headed by Dave House, with a strong focus on supplying building blocks such as processors, chip sets, caches, motherboards, and systems. When House left Intel in 1996 to become CEO of Bay Networks, John Minor became the new general manager and led our efforts to serve this important and growing market.

In addition to the fast-growing server market, we also saw opportunities in the very important workstation market. Processing requirements in that market include high-performance mathematics functions, like floating point, and fast processor-to-memory communications to handle intense graphics applications. When we were developing the Pentium Pro processor (described in Chapter 10), we kept these requirements in mind. We invented a number of innovative technologies to dramatically improve the performance of the Pentium Pro and Pentium II processors for the workstation and server markets, as well as for the desktop and mobile segments. The new Dynamic Execution technology made the processor run even faster and boosted the floating-point performance of the chip by more than a factor of two over that of the Pentium processor. To boost the communication speed between processor and memory, the team invented a completely new bus structure called the Dual Independent Bus (DIB). The DIB consists of two buses: one in back to handle dedicated and fast communications between the processor and the cache memory, and one in front to handle fast communications between the processor and the main memory and other processors.

The combination of Dynamic Execution and the Dual Independent Bus made the Pentium Pro processor even better than the Pentium processor for building high-performance workstations and servers. When the Pentium Pro processor was introduced in 1995, it became an instant hit with our workstation and server customers. Coupled with the Microsoft Windows NT* operating system, the Pentium Pro processor became the heart of workstation offerings from companies such as Compaq, IBM, Dell, Netpower, and many others. These Intel architecture/Windows NT products offered much better price–performance than UNIX*/RISC workstations. Intel formed a Workstation Products Division in early 1997 to focus on serving this growing market.

Even while we were developing the Pentium Pro processor, we realized that to expand our business into the workstation and server markets, we had to jump to microprocessors that address 64 bits at a time—twice as fast as the 32-bit processor. We also needed to expand the speed of communications between the processor and the memory system to handle the increasingly high demand of fast transaction processing for complex server applications. We started our 64-bit development effort in 1992 and came up with many good ideas. We decided very early on that we wanted to take a giant step forward in defining the 64-bit architecture so that it would satisfy the market requirements for years to come—well into the twenty-first century. We knew we had to have a product line that was software compatible and capable of running all the existing 32-bit software for the Intel architecture. It had to have high performance and high-memory bandwidth. And we needed to make it scalable with lots of head room to expand its capability well into the future. John Crawford, one of our most experienced architects, was put in charge of this effort.

Late in 1993, we discovered that Hewlett-Packard had been doing extensive research on 64-bit computing as well. They realized that their RISC Precision Architecture would soon run out of steam, and they needed something much better. They also realized that they could not economically justify having their own RISC processor developments just for themselves, and they wanted to switch to a commercial processor, such as the Intel microprocessor, to satisfy their enterprise computing requirements. Our discussions with HP led to the discovery that their architectural research work and ours were complementary. We realized that if we were to join forces in defining

*Trademark

the 64-bit instruction set, we could come up with the breakthrough technology that would be the architectural standard for all high-end computing well into the next decade. It was an exciting opportunity for both of us. We immediately discussed further how we could work closely together.

By June of 1994, we announced that we had formed an alliance to define the 64-bit technology. Intel would design, produce, and sell the resultant microprocessor products to all our customers and HP would focus on building their future system products based on this new microprocessor family. It was a win-win for both sides. We put our best talents together to define the best 64-bit architecture for workstations and servers. The 64-bit instruction set work was completed by 1995 and we started to design several microprocessor products with this technology. We came up with an exciting technology called EPIC (Explicitly Parallel Instruction Computer) which took a giant step beyond the superscalar technology to gain much higher performance. We hope to have the first of these new products, called Merced, into the marketplace in the next few years, and to further expand our product road map for workstations and servers.

Starting with a modest product line of two 386 products in 1985, Intel's product road map today encompasses all segments of the computing market, from mobile to desktop to workstations to servers. As the market segments even further—from high-end servers to basic PCs for business to high-performance multimedia PCs to TV set-top computers in the home—we are expanding our product offerings to serve this broadening market. We offer a compelling product road map of building blocks for the computing industry that includes processors, chip sets, caches, motherboards, and systems for our customers to build, sell, and service their complete computer offerings—from top to bottom.

The secret of a great business is great products. Specifically, a successful high-technology company has to define, develop, and deliver a clear, ever-improving product road map that exceeds market expectations over

an extended period of time. It took us many years to build such a road map from a modest base. Now we have a constantly improving and expanding road map that encompasses all segments of the PC market from mobiles to desktops to workstations to servers, for business and consumer applications. The key is to understand clearly the different requirements of each market segment and then to tailor products for these segments. We learn and experiment along the way. We aim to provide all of the building blocks that the computer industry needs: microprocessors, chip sets, caches, communication products, motherboards, and systems. We have taken risks, stumbled, and learned along the way. We keep at it with the strong conviction that the next product will be much better than the last. As a result, our product road map keeps getting better and broader.

CHAPTER FIVE

COLLABORATE WITH CUSTOMERS AND COMPLEMENTORS

WHO ARE OUR CUSTOMERS?

A SIMPLE QUESTION, RIGHT? NOT NECESSARILY. IF YOU MANUFACTURE automobile engines, your customers are automobile manufacturers such as General Motors (GM) and Ford. If you're GM, your customers are all the GM dealers selling your cars, but mostly the consumers who buy and drive your cars. While the customer buys his car from a dealer, he knows that he is driving a GM car and looks to GM to stand behind it.

When Intel started out in the semiconductor memory business, our customer relationships were very straightforward. Our customers were computer manufacturers. We dealt with these companies' engineering and purchasing departments through our field sales engineers (called FSEs at Intel).

Once we entered the microprocessor business, defining our customer became more complex. As I mentioned in Chapter 2, in addition to addressing engineering and purchasing departments, we needed to also address the CEOs of our customers. We needed to assure high-level executives that we had a long-term product road map that would satisfy their strategic long-term needs. A company's selection of microprocessors was more of a strategic decision than its selection of memory or other products. In addition, because designing microprocessor-based systems was a fairly complex technical job, Intel set up in the 1970s a new team of specialists, called field application engineers (FAEs), who gave technical support to our customers' engineering staffs. This was a new and innovative concept at the time and one that helped our customers design better and faster microprocessor-based systems.

When our customers get products to market quickly and sell them in high volumes, we benefit by having more microprocessor sales—clearly a win-win situation for all. Also, because our FAEs are in continuous contact with technical personnel at our customer sites, they are in an excellent position to talk to them about new Intel products. They also gather valuable feedback on what features the customers really want in our products and how we might improve them. Field sales engineers normally form strong links to purchasing people and handle the business aspects of the relationship. Field application engineers, on the other hand, typically establish strong rapport with the system design engineers. For years, we were the only company with FAEs helping customers, which gave us a tremendous advantage in supporting and influencing our customers. We set up regular communications between our FAEs and our chip designers to incorporate customer inputs into our next-generation products.

ADDRESS OUR CUSTOMERS' CUSTOMERS

During the early stages of promoting the 386 processor in the late 1980s, we worked hard with our traditional customers—PC manufacturers—to get them to use the 386 in their product lines. A number of upstarts such as Compaq, Acer, and others, jumped on the 386 opportunity. However, we were surprised to receive a lukewarm reception from IBM, the PC market leader and trendsetter. They had decided that the 286 was good enough and would serve their needs for a long time. The situation was very frustrating for us. Without

IBM's strong endorsement, how could we move the market to the newer and better 386?

Dennis Carter, then Andy Grove's technical assistant, came up with the idea of addressing PC end users directly about the virtues of the 386. This was a novel and risky concept at the time. It was like an engine manufacturer addressing car drivers directly about the virtues of the engine inside their cars. We had never dealt directly with end users before. Besides, our customers, PC manufacturers, might not like us addressing their customers directly. Still, we reasoned that because the microprocessor defined the performance and characteristics of the PC, it was appropriate for us to educate end users as to why they should buy newer and faster 386 PCs rather than older and slower 286 machines. The result was Intel's "Red X" campaign, aimed directly at PC users. We ran an ad with a big red X over the 286, and a strong message, "Now, get 386 system performance at a 286 system price." (For more details about this campaign, see Chapter 10, "Obsolete our Own Products.") The ad campaign was a great success—end users rushed to buy 386-based PCs, and 386 sales

FIGURE 7A   THE RED X CAMPAIGN

Source: Intel

FIGURE 7B   THE INFLUENCE MAP

Source: Intel

took off. Addressing end users directly was a watershed event for Intel. We realized that our customers were not only PC manufacturers but also the end users that bought PCs.

Once we knew that our customers included end users, several logical steps followed. We mounted the "Intel Inside" advertising campaign, which successfully established the Intel brand name in consumers' minds. In concert with this consumer ad campaign, we worked with our primary customers, PC manufacturers, to encourage them to display the "Intel Inside" symbol in their ads and on their products. We worked hard over many years to execute this campaign, and it was extremely successful all over the world.

ESTABLISH LINKS TO CORPORATE CUSTOMERS

Our second major effort at establishing end-customer links was directed at corporate chief information officers (CIOs), the people who manage the computer operations in major corporations. They typically decide what computer technology is deployed within their companies. They are obviously very influential and represent the "super end user," as each CIO represents thousands of users. These big buyers are in constant touch with computer company suppliers. With technology advancing so rapidly, they are eager to hear from us directly about new technology and products.

In 1993, we set up advisory boards in the United States (and later in Europe, Japan, and Asia Pacific) with key CIOs from leading companies such as Ford, Boeing, Chase Manhattan, and others. We meet with these boards quarterly and present our products, technology, and future plans. The gatherings are mutually beneficial: the CIOs get valuable information on our future products and technology directions, and we get valuable inputs on their needs, their suggestions, and their feedback about our products.

In one of these sessions in 1996, CIOs made it clear that their number-one challenge was to reduce the total cost of ownership of PCs—not just the purchase price, but the ongoing cost of maintaining, upgrading, and fixing networked PCs. Because of this strong input, we formed an industry initiative to drive down total cost with technologies such as remote diagnostics and remote repair of PCs and servers. We not only have aggressive programs ourselves but work with other partners on this important task. For example, we work closely with IBM in sharing manageability technology and with Microsoft on a specification that dramatically reduces the cost of PC ownership: the NetPC. In fact, we worked with the entire PC industry to develop the NetPC specification as well as the product. We launched the NetPC products with Microsoft and many of our PC customers at the June 1997 PC Expo. These products, which address an important need for corporate customers, were very well received at the introduction.

In addition to establishing a dialog with key CIOs, we have worked to make ourselves available with the CIOs' staffs in information technology (IT) organizations. IT professionals are anxious to get the latest product and technology information from Intel so they can select the right technology for their organizations. In response to their needs, we set up an organization of architecture managers (AMs), whose job is not to sell products but rather to provide timely information and support for corporate IT organizations. Their role is similar to that of the FAEs, who provide technical information and support for our OEMs' system design engineers. Neither of these Intel organizations sells products directly, but both provide an extremely important function in explaining our advanced and fast-changing product road map to IT and OEM customers and supporting them fully. Just like the field application engineers, architecture managers are also an effective vehicle in getting direct feedback from the IT people on how to improve our products and what new products they need.

HELP THE CHANNELS SELL TO END USERS

As Intel assumed the task of staying close to end users, we had to understand the channels through which end users buy PCs. Consumers purchase their PCs from many different channels, including retail computer stores, computer superstores, direct order, World Wide Web, and resellers. We realized that we needed to provide support to all these channels so they could better serve end users. In retail environments, serving customers well means providing clear displays on the latest products, having the right products available, and making sure that salespeople are knowledgeable about the latest offerings.

During the fall of 1994, when multimedia home PCs began to become really popular, some of us visited a number of leading retail stores. Some were doing really well. They were well stocked with Pentium processor–based PCs and had excellent in-store displays and knowledgeable salespeople on the floor. But we also found that many were not doing so well. They were still carrying older 486 processor–based systems that did not run multimedia applications well. Salespeople were not knowledgeable about the virtues of Pentium processor–based systems and knew very little about the new, exciting multimedia applications.

There was a clear correlation between having the latest, greatest products on the floor, with salespeople who were excited about them, and how well a store did in PC sales.

We immediately set up a team of Retail Managers to work with key retail and computer superstores across the United States. Our goal was to help retail stores sell Pentium processor–based PCs more effectively. We staged "demo days," where Intel put up colorful displays describing the benefits of Pentium processor–based PCs and gave live demonstrations of exciting multimedia applications. These events were heavily promoted by the retailers and drew many consumers who were anxious to see the latest thing and talk directly with Intel people about the Pentium processor. Typically, sales of Pentium processor–based PCs jumped by a factor of three to five during these events and continued at a brisk pace if the store staff continued giving demos and showing enthusiasm for these products. The Christmas 1994 season turned out to be a great one for Pentium processor–based PC sales, and demo days certainly helped by establishing a model of successful retailing. Since then, our Retail Managers have continued to work closely with key retailers to tailor store displays to Intel processor–based PCs and to support the sales staff with the latest product and technology information. It is a win-win situation, as the stores enjoy better sales, PC OEMs get added support, and Intel benefits by getting higher volumes of the latest processor into the market faster.

COLLABORATE WITH COMPLEMENTORS

Intel supplies critical parts of the PC hardware: the microprocessor, the chip set, cache memory, and graphics chips. PC manufacturers build PCs with our chips, plus many other hardware components—memory, hard disk drives, monitors, and so on. End users buy not only the PC hardware but also software products from companies like Microsoft, Intuit, Adobe, and others, to run their applications. While Intel does not buy or sell products from these independent hardware vendors (IHVs) and independent software vendors (ISVs), these companies clearly complement us in providing a total PC product for end users. I believe the term complementor[14] describes this relationship well.

Our relationship with Microsoft provides a perfect example. IBM adopted Microsoft's DOS as the operating system for its first PC and our 8088 microprocessor as the core hardware. The operating system and the microprocessor became the pillars of the modern-day PC. As a result, we have worked closely with Microsoft on a wide variety of technical matters to advance the technology of the PC. During 1987 and 1988, Microsoft was engaged in a joint development project with IBM to build the OS/2 operating system that was to run on the Intel 286 processor. We approached Microsoft to explain the virtues of the 386, telling them that we thought the 386 was where the PC industry was heading. They instantly saw the benefits of that chip's higher performance and the opportunity to build new and exciting software to take advantage of it. This began a much closer working relationship between Intel and Microsoft. We started having regular meetings to exchange information on our respective technologies, customer requirements, and product directions.

When Intel first invented MMX technology for the Pentium processor, we showed Microsoft its benefits for multimedia applications and received enthusiastic support from their operating systems, tools, and applications groups. We did the same with many other ISVs, including Adobe, Macromedia, Avid, and others. Because of our close cooperation with Microsoft and other ISVs, MMX technology–ready applications were on the market when we announced the Pentium processor with MMX technology. Thanks to this kind of industry-wide cooperation, the Pentium processor with MMX technology has been one of the most successful products we have ever launched.

Industry collaborations typically benefit all parties. Microsoft's Windows version 3.0 ran slowly on the 386 but much better on the more powerful 486 processor. This served to make both the Windows 3.0 operating system and the 486 processor extremely successful. Our fast processors consistently make software run better and faster, which benefits both end users and ISVs. This cycle of product improvement results in a win-win situation for all concerned.

Intel works closely with many software companies to ensure that their software takes full advantage of the performance and features we put into our processors and the latest PC systems. To strengthen our working relationships and cooperation with these companies, we set up a team of Strategic Software Technical Managers (SSTMs). These individuals keep key software companies updated on our products and technology directions. They also understand where these companies are going and gather their inputs on what we need to incorporate in our processors and chip sets to help their software run better. We arrange executive-level meetings with ISVs to exchange ideas and ensure that our products work well together. In many cases, we treat our complementors like customers, because we depend on them so heavily. The increasing importance of our relationship with software and content company collaborators led us to form a Content Group in 1996 under Senior Vice President Ron Whittier. The group has spearheaded our efforts to work more closely with companies to expand optimized content titles for both consumer and business markets.

PC manufacturers buy microprocessors and chip sets from Intel and other suppliers. But they also buy memories, graphics chips, disk controllers, communications chips, hard disks, and other hardware components from independent hardware vendors (IHVs). It is to our mutual benefit that we exchange ideas with IHVs on where the industry is going and support one another in designing complementary products. For example, we visit memory companies such as Samsung, NEC, Toshiba, and Hitachi on a regular basis to exchange market data and product directions. As we understand each other better, we can work together to get our processors to work better with their memory products. As PC voltage and power requirements change over time, we visit power supply companies to exchange product and technical information also. These are just a few examples of our proactive work with many IHVs so that our products will work better together.

DRIVE INDUSTRY TECHNOLOGY INITIATIVES

The high-technology industry consists of many constituents that are closely linked either through direct buying and selling relationships or in some form of collaborative relationship. Yet everyone in the industry depends on one another to grow and prosper together, like members in an "ecosystem."[15] Figure 8 shows how Intel interacts with its customers, complementors, and others, and how we influence each other. As you can see, we have proactively put together a number of organizations to work with each of these important groups of people.

In 1989, as we were working to improve and advance the PC platform, we realized that we needed to involve all our key OEM customers and hardware and software complementors to move in a common direction. We came up with the idea of holding a technology forum and inviting one to two hundred executives from our OEM customers and key complementor companies. In our first forum, held in San Francisco in June 1990, we shared our future technology and product directions and got their feedback in defining the direction of the PC platform. It was a great session, with a lot of good interactions and exchange of ideas. We all came to a clear, common conclusion: multiprocessing would be important in the future in order to build scalable systems. As a result, Intel designed key multiprocessing features in our Pentium and Pentium Pro processors and the associated chip sets. Many of the companies who attended that forum have developed their own multiprocessing products. This started an industry trend toward multiprocessing that greatly benefits the users by offering better price performance and more scalable systems.

In 1991, we held a second technology forum, where the issue of the day was improving or replacing the old ISA bus. The new PCI bus was the key topic. Everybody was excited about moving to this

FIGURE 8   THE INFLUENCE MAP

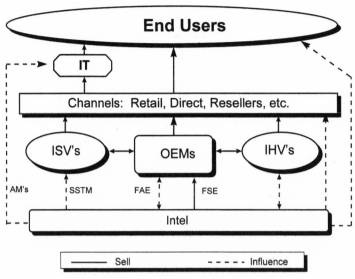

Source: Intel

new bus to boost PC performance from the old PC-AT of 1984. In addition to encouraging the industry to move toward the PCI bus at that forum, I was able to demonstrate a software simulation of our superscalar technology for the Pentium processor, then in development. Not only was the audience surprised to see that Intel's next-generation processor technology was so close at hand, but they were very impressed with the demonstration of superscalar technology that would propel the Pentium processor to the head of the class in performance.

At the third forum, in December 1992, the topics discussed were much broader. We invited many speakers, from Pacific Gas & Electric, Microsoft, IBM, and other industry leaders, to address key PC issues. It became clear at this forum that the PC market was broadening into many segments, each with a number of different requirements. Many PC companies were realigning their organizations to better serve these distinct markets. As a result, Intel decided to expand its product road map to serve desktop, mobile, and server segments and to similarly realign its organization to better serve these expanding markets.

In 1995, the theme of our technology forum was "Growing the Market," and we discussed such topics as connectivity, multimedia applications, ease of use, manageability, and scalability. The aim of this forum was to get the whole PC industry to work together to grow the total market. We came up with concrete programs to make the PC easier to use and to develop better multimedia hardware and software. The industry excitement over multimedia applications reinforced our dedicated efforts in developing the Pentium processor with MMX technology.

As the emerging markets in Asia and other regions discovered the wonders of the PC, the sales of our chips grew very rapidly in these regions. As these markets became bigger and more important, we expanded our technology forums into Asia. More than 100 key PC industry executives attended our first Asian forum in Hong Kong, in May 1996. It was a great event. Seeing our latest technology and product directions helped the audience set their own product direction. We also gained good insights into the local PC market and valuable inputs on what our Asian customers wanted. In May 1997, we held our second such session, in Taipei, Taiwan, with close to 300 attendees. Key people from the local PC industry were there mapping out the future in an open environment where ideas could be debated and explored with an eye to what was best for the entire industry—as well as their own companies. This free flow of ideas is one of the key reasons why the PC and other high-technology industries innovate and advance so quickly.

By late 1995, the PC market had grown enormously, and its impact on the business world had increased many-fold. The Internet phenomenon had gathered huge momentum in the commercial arena, dramatically accelerating the public's interest in computing. We felt we needed to expand our relatively small technology forum audiences to include members of the press, industry analysts, and even the public. The press and financial and technology analysts have always been key players in our industry. They have enormous influence in shaping the opinions of end users and other industry players. As a public company, Intel briefs the financial and analyst community on its business directions and financial performance on a routine basis. Thus evolved our first public technology forum: the Internet Media Symposium, held in March 1996 in San Mateo, California. More than 1,300 people showed up to hear representatives from Intel, Sony Music, @Home, NBC, Macromedia, Adobe, and other Internet leaders talk about the future of the Internet and exciting Internet applications.

The second technology symposium was held in September 1996 in New York City. The central topic was "Wired for Management," and attendees addressed the important issues of reducing the cost of owning and managing PCs. Key executives from IBM, HP, and Computer Associates shared with the audience their visions of how to advance key management issues. Both of these events generated strong industry momentum toward generating exciting Internet applications and developing technologies and products that resulted in reducing the total cost of PC ownership.

In 1997, we held two more public forums, beginning with a symposium on Visual Computing in March 1997 in Santa Clara. There, many speakers discussed how the PC of the future would have enough power to enable "visual computing," incorporating video, 3D, and digital imaging. Intel's aim was to marshal the whole industry to make the PC the best visual computing platform and to generate exciting business and consumer applications for the new platform. More than 60 software companies demonstrated exciting visual software on Intel architecture platforms, and more than 1,300 people attended the conference. We held our second symposium, entitled "Visual Connected PCs—The Next Business Computing Platform," on June 2, 1997, in New York City, with about 1,500 people in attendance. Intel, many customers, and complementors demonstrated that the next frontier of business computing would take full advantage of PC graphics and video capabilities that would make Internet business transactions fast and simple. The audience was delighted to see demonstrations of leading-edge software that featured innovative visual capabilities such as video and 3D.

These technology forums have been very effective avenues for addressing major industry initiatives and demonstrating forward-looking technologies and applications. They're also great opportunities for key players to talk, debate, and innovate together. These gatherings are invaluable for keeping the whole industry vibrant and dynamic.

There are many ways to cooperate and interact with customers and complementors—one-on-one meetings, small group sessions, and large industry events. More recently, the World Wide Web has emerged as an important medium for communicating with our audiences: OEMs, software developers, hardware developers, IT people, PC channels, financial and industry analysts and, of course, PC end users. Our Web site gives everyone instant access to the latest information on Intel products and technology, and news of technology forums and seminars. We also offer special Web pages to supply our distributors and resellers with information they need for their businesses. We have been constantly improving our Web site with a better user interface, better and more content, and more powerful servers for faster response time. We now conduct electronic sales and marketing and electronic commerce on the Web. It is amazing to think that this new World Wide Web technology was made possible in the first place by the widespread use of PCs. It provides us with the best possible interactive medium for getting in touch with all our customers and partners around the world.

Those of us in the high-technology industry must do a great job for all our customers and complementors—manufacturers, hardware developers, software developers, and end users. We need to support each group with technical and product information so they can design better PCs and help end users make more intelligent buying decisions. We need to support all the channels that serve our end customers.

With technology moving so quickly, one of our key activities is collaborating with both customers and complementors to ensure that they take full advantage of our products and technology. We work very closely with our complementors to make sure our products work well together and result in better, faster, cheaper PCs. The high-technology digital industry is a vibrant and living system with all participants innovating and challenging each other to do a better job for end users.

CHAPTER SIX

DRIVE FOR
HIGH VOLUME

ONE OF THE KEYS TO A SUCCESSFUL HIGH-TECHNOLOGY BUSINESS IS TO deliver newer and better products in rapidly rising volume to satisfy customer demand. Volume and speed are critical. Why is volume so important? High-volume production drives down manufacturing costs. High volume also translates into high revenues. The combination of high revenues and low cost generates the profits needed to fund the technology development that keeps the whole high-technology cycle going. Also, the highest-volume product tends to set the trend that the rest of the industry follows. Why is speed so important? As technology advances according to Moore's Law, you must be fast enough to keep up with the pace. If you are late to market by a year or more, you have just missed a whole product generation and have to start all over again. It's like riding a bicycle: if you don't peddle and move forward quickly, you will fall.

VOLUME IS KING

According to Dataquest, total PC shipments are expected to exceed 100 million units worldwide in 1998. This is a huge number. It's more than the total number of cars produced worldwide (about 20 million per year) by a wide margin, and it approaches the total number of televisions sold worldwide. It took the television about 50 years to reach this kind of volume, but it took the PC less than a third of that

FIGURE 9 PC MARKET GROWTH

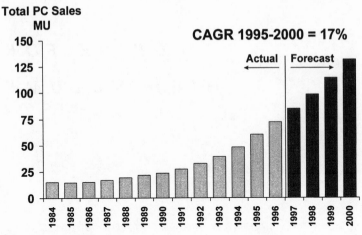

Source: Dataquest '97

time. What fueled this phenomenal rise in volume has been the incredible outpouring of new and exciting hardware and software products in rapidly rising volume to feed a hungry marketplace.

ECONOMICS OF THE SEMICONDUCTOR BUSINESS

Back in 1972, we decided to convert our wafer fabrication facility from one that used two-inch silicon wafers to one that used three-inch wafers for building our memory products. Why was this such an important change? First of all, a three-inch wafer has more than twice the surface area of a two-inch wafer and therefore can host more than twice as many memory chips. This is good, as it doubles the output from essentially the same manufacturing space (manufacturing capacity is more a function of the number of wafers than the wafer's size).

Second, the manufacturing cost for a three-inch wafer is only slightly higher than that for a two-inch wafer. Therefore, in a three-inch facility, the cost of a chip drops by about half. We get twice the output at half the cost! Of course, we have to buy bigger and more expensive manufacturing equipment to process the larger wafers. But it is still a highly profitable move, since the increase in volume and the much lower chip costs more than make up for the higher equip-ment costs.

Another critical production factor in the semiconductor industry is *yield*. The yield of a wafer is the number of good chips divided by the total number of chips available on a wafer. The reason yield is not 100 percent is because there are invariably manufacturing de-fects that render some of the chips unusable. In fact, in the early days of semiconductor manufacturing, yield was extremely low—only a few percentage points per wafer. The science and art of achieving high yields lies at the heart of semiconductor manufacturing tech-nology. If you can improve your manufacturing processes to elimi-nate defects, you can dramatically improve yield, which raises output and reduces costs.

In converting our manufacturing process from two-inch to three-inch wafers, our number-one focus was to improve the yield on the new three-inch technology. We worked day and night to develop a three-inch process that gave us not only two times more output due to wafer size increase, but also another 50 percent increase on output due to yield improvements. This resulted in a threefold increase in output and three times lower cost. That very successful effort boosted our 1103 memory output dramatically and lowered the cost at the same time. We had a very profitable year in 1973 and became the leader in memory products. During this same time, a Canadian com-petitor, MIL, attempted the same wafer conversion but failed and went into bankruptcy.

Let me give you some examples of how wafer size and yields im-pact profitability. Assume that a two-inch wafer costs $100 to pro-duce, and the yield is 20 percent. Out of 100 chips per wafer, you have 20 good chips to sell. That means each of those 20 chips cost $5 to produce (for this simple example, I will assume that packaging costs for the chip are negligible). If you sell them for $7 each, that makes your revenue per wafer $140 ($7 times 20) and your profit per wafer $40 ($2 times 20).

For three-inch wafers, let's say that your production cost is $120 per wafer. The total of available chips would be 225, because the area is bigger. Assume that the yield is improved to 30 percent. Therefore, each wafer yields 67 (30 percent of 225) salable chips, each of which costs only $1.80 ($120 divided by 67) to manufacture. Now your revenue per wafer jumps to $469 ($7 times 67) and your profit per wafer jumps to $348 ($5.20 times 67)! Dramatic, isn't it? However, let's say that during the three-inch conversion, the yield crashed to 5 percent with everything else staying the same. Now, with only 11 good chips per wafer, costs would jump to about $11. As the selling price of a good chip was still $7, revenue per wafer would drop to only $77 ($7 times 11), a loss of $44 ($4 times 11) per wafer—clearly a disaster. This shows the dramatic impact of yield in semiconductor economics.

As you can see, the critical profit equation in the semiconductor business involves a combination of good yield and larger wafer size to generate high outputs and low costs. Intel has successfully moved from three- to four- to six- to eight-inch wafers, engineering dramatic yield improvements along the way, so that our factories today run at extremely high yields. The result is high-volume output at low cost, the key to semiconductor business success. We are not alone. Other semiconductor companies drive for high yields and large wafer-size production for exactly the same reasons.

VOLUME IS THE KEY FOR SOFTWARE

The economics of the software business are very different from those of semiconductor production, but achieving high volume is still paramount. Manufacturing and capital costs are minimal for software. It costs very little to copy a software product onto a disk or CD and even less to make it available over the World Wide Web. As a result, the product margin (the difference between price and cost) is very close to the revenue. Therefore, both the revenue and product margin rise with increasing product volume.

Let's say that there are 200 million PCs out there. If one software product sells to 20 percent of the market at a price of $20, it generates revenues and product margins of $800 million, a very large sum that could fund lots of new product development and marketing efforts. However, if another software product garners only 1 percent of the market, it earns revenues and product margins of only $40 million. The development costs for these two products might be the same, but the revenues and profits earned would be dramatically different because of the differences in volume sold. In this example, if development costs were $40 million, the first company would earn profit of $760 million, but the second company would just break even.

The fact that the material and manufacturing costs for software are minimal is the basis of a totally different business model where achieving high volume is even more critical. Microsoft pioneered the volume strategy for software by offering a very low price for its original DOS operating system, which quickly became the volume leader and the de facto standard as the operating system for the PC market. MS-DOS became the only operating system that software vendors developed application software for. Microsoft was also extremely successful in developing application software products such as Microsoft Word, Microsoft Excel, and Microsoft PowerPoint, on top of its operating system. In the process, Microsoft became the leading software company, reaping profits from relatively low-priced, but high-volume products.

More recently, one of the common strategies in the software business is to go one step further and give away the initial product for free, with the hope of establishing a large installed base upon which future upgrades and associated applications and add-ons can be sold. Netscape Communications pioneered this strategy with its Netscape Navigator, a browser for the World Wide Web. By giving away the early versions of

Navigator, they quickly became the volume leader in the Internet market. They then sold upgrades and other products on top of it and built a very strong, high-volume business. Many other software companies are following the same strategy to drive for high volume.

Another example is the PC game market. Game console manufacturers sell their hardware game consoles at very low prices with hopes of establishing a very high-volume installed base. Most of the profits are then made by selling large volumes of game software to that installed base. If there are 10 million units of game console A out there, and each owner is likely to buy 10 software games, the market for the game software is 100 million units. However, if game console B only has 1 million units in the field and each owner again will buy 10 software games, the market is only 10 million units. Thus game manufacturers aim to sell lots of inexpensive consoles so they can sell large volumes of game software with higher profit margins. This is exactly the same strategy as selling lots of razor blades to a large number of razor owners. Volume is king.

HIGH VOLUME DEMANDS HIGH QUALITY

To achieve high-volume production, the product must be of high quality. High-volume production is very difficult if one has lots of rejects. The only way to achieve high volume is to truly engineer the product for quality right from the beginning so that it can be manufactured, tested, and shipped to customers smoothly and rapidly. To run high-volume semiconductor production, one must combine high yield with low defects in the manufacturing process. One must design into the manufacturing system high quality and low defects right from the beginning.

DESIGN QUALITY IN THE BEGINNING

The principle of designing in quality is simple and well-known, but Intel learned this lesson the hard way. In 1974, when the semiconductor industry was going through a recession, Intel asked me to join the reliability engineering group to solve some of the nagging problems we were having with our memory products. It was a difficult job, particularly as we were trying to solve these reliability problems as production was ramping up. Several times, I had to shut down the line so we could fix problems. We had lots of quality assurance (QA) inspectors examining for quality both on the production line and at the end of the line. Many products had to be scrapped, and this was extremely expensive for us. We soon realized that instead of fighting fires, we had to approach the problem differently. We had to understand the root causes of the quality problems and fix them at the source. We had to make sure quality and reliability were designed into the products right from the beginning rather than being "inspected in" during production.

As we pushed the state of the art in semiconductor technology by making everything smaller, we were also pushing the reliability limits. For example, as the oxide of metal oxide semiconductor (MOS) devices became ever thinner, current was more likely to leak through the oxide, causing reliability problems. Therefore, in order to build smaller but reliable MOS transistors, we needed to solve the associated technical problems. This required detailed knowledge of device physics, material science, and reliability engineering. Realizing the importance of reliability, my colleague Gerry Parker and I, built a world-class team of reliability engineers to understand reliability physics and to ensure that new silicon technologies and products incorporated the best reliability requirements right from the beginning of development.

Ensuring that the product and technology are developed with clear reliability and quality goals from the very start is easy to talk about but difficult to do. In 1974, we set out to move quality and reliability engineers onto every product and technology development team at Intel. This organizational change really paid off. For example, we discovered that most of our plastics reliability problems were due to excessive phosphorous in the thin films covering the chip.

The presence of reliability engineers on the technology development teams resulted in new technologies that produced much less phosphorous and much higher reliability. In another example, reliability engineers also make sure that all the metal interconnects are designed with sufficient width to sustain the needed electrical current over the lifetime of the chip. Making quality and reliability an integral and fundamental requirement of product design was critical in enabling microprocessor and memory production to ramp to millions and millions of units per year with little or no QA inspection and rework.

From the inception of the company, Andy Grove insisted that Intel products have the best quality and reliability in the industry. Craig Barrett, Intel's president; Gerry Parker, Intel executive vice president; and I all ran Intel's quality and reliability organization early in our careers. Quality is a key pillar of Intel's culture, as I will discuss in the next chapter.

As we moved from memory products to microprocessors, we discovered that the physics of the semiconductor remained the same, but the product complexity increased dramatically, pushing us to expand our quality frontier. A unique quality challenge for microprocessor makers is to ensure that the chip correctly runs all possible combinations of the instructions. We put our chips through an extensive validation process to make certain that they will operate properly. This validation effort becomes more difficult, as today's complex chips have millions of transistors. In fact, it is impossible to check all possible combinations of instructions, as there is an infinite number of them. We must have a comprehensive validation program to make sure that our microprocessors work with all the software products, as well as all possible PC configurations. This has become a daunting task as the products get more complex and the number of software and hardware combinations increases. However, PC users demand the highest quality, which we must deliver. Software companies share a similar challenge. Complex software products such as Microsoft Windows, Intuit's Quicken, and Netscape Navigator must be free of serious bugs that impact end-users. For these software products, the solution to a bug can be a simple software patch available through the World Wide Web or on disk. For silicon products such as microprocessors, most errata can also be "worked around" through software solutions. For others, a design fix is necessary. This naturally takes more time and is very expensive. Therefore, the quality and validation requirements for silicon products are even more stringent than those for software.

Since the 286 days in the early 1980s, Intel has had processor validation teams focus on testing the widest possible variety of software and hardware combinations. We discovered several errata in the 386 and 486 processors that caused the chips to operate improperly under certain conditions. By working closely with our OEM customers and software companies, we developed workarounds to ensure that these errata did not impact end-users. We significantly increased our validation efforts to catch errata before chips entered volume production. Little did we know that we had yet to learn a big lesson about how to handle errata with end-users.

THE FDIV LESSON

In the summer of 1994, as we were ramping production of the Pentium processors, we found an erratum in the floating-point section of the chip during our ongoing validation process. We immediately assigned a team to analyze the problem and its impact. The team found that under certain conditions a small error could result that was associated with the floating-point divide (FDIV)[16] instruction. The affected type of calculation was performed primarily in scientific applications, a small percentage of the Pentium processor market. Our engineers found that the error occurred very rarely and had minimal impact on most end-users. We decided that it was not significant enough to our customers to warrant recalling the product. We also found the root cause of the erratum, fixed it, and put the corrected product into production. At the same time, we continued to analyze different applications in the scientific area to find worst-case impacts of the erratum; still, we found little impact.

That fall, a professor of mathematics at Lynchburg College in Virginia, Thomas Nicely, who had been using the Pentium processor instead of supercomputers in his research on prime numbers, found subtle differences between the results from his Pentium processor–based systems and a 486 processor–based system. He could not find anyone at Intel to respond to his discovery, as we were ill equipped to handle individual inquiries at the time. (Since then, we have dramatically improved our telephone and Internet response systems for handling end-user inquiries.) He decided to post his findings on the Internet, showing a formula that demonstrated the discrepancy.

Immediately, people on the Internet jumped on the "Pentium processor flaw," and the news spread. Many end-users called Intel directly, asking if their PCs were OK. Some demanded replacement chips. We pulled lots of people from their jobs to answer the phones, because we had little experience and insufficient staff for dealing directly with end-users. We explained our technical findings to these callers and said we would replace their chips if their applications involved heavy floating-point calculations. This response was not well received.

On November 22, 1994, CNN carried a worldwide story saying that the Pentium processor had a flaw, and the press rushed in. Calls and Internet stories exploded, and we pulled hundreds more people away from their normal duties to handle the flood of phone calls. People worked day and night all the way through the Thanksgiving holidays to handle the inquiries. Most of our OEM customers and software companies, such as Microsoft, were very supportive of our position that the erratum was insignificant. However, on December 12, IBM announced that it would stop shipping PCs containing "flawed" Pentium processors, and this triggered a big panic in the marketplace.

After much intense internal discussion and debate about what to do, we finally realized that whether or not we thought the erratum was significant was not important. Our end-customers thought it was, and that was all that mattered. We had to replace chips with no questions asked, assuring consumers that Intel stood behind its products. On December 21, 1994, we ran an ad in the *Wall Street Journal* that said, "We at Intel wish to sincerely apologize for our handling of the recently publicized Pentium processor flaw. The Intel Inside® symbol means that your computer has a microprocessor second to none in quality and performance. Thousands of Intel employees work very hard to ensure that this is true. But no microprocessor is ever perfect. . . . Intel will exchange the current version of the Pentium processor for an updated version, in which this floating-point divide flaw is corrected, for any owner who requests it, free of charge anytime during the life of the computer. . . . "

It was a painful rite of passage, but we had finally learned how to behave like a consumer company. With that announcement, the public and the press calmed down and praised us for doing the right thing. We took a huge financial charge of $475 million for this enormous lesson. The whole company worked around the clock through the Christmas season and beyond to handle all the details of replacing the chips. It was an exhausting and painful experience for all of us.

Intel held big "thank you" events for employees around the world in appreciation for all who worked so hard to deal with this huge crisis. As a memento, everyone got a Pentium processor key chain with the inscription, "Bad companies are destroyed by crisis. Good companies survive them. Great companies are improved by them. Andy Grove, December 1994."

Intel not only survived this crisis but was made stronger by it. First, we learned yet again that quality is number one. I have since driven my team to dramatically improve our validation methodology to quickly capture and fix errata. We also have investigated many innovative ways to design products that are error-free right from the beginning. Second, we learned that the privilege of addressing end-users directly through our advertising and retail contacts brings with it the responsibility of listening and responding to them directly when they have problems. To do this, we set up permanent phone support teams and Web-based discussion groups to listen to and respond to consumer needs. Third, enduring this crisis made our worldwide team work together much more closely. We found we could shorten our response time from days to minutes on urgent matters. We developed trust between many different groups in solving problems and marching in the same direction. Lastly, we embarked on a policy to publish all errata we found so that our end-users would have open and full disclosure from us. We explain all errata to OEMs and ISVs and work with them to devise workarounds so that there is minimal impact on end-users. Interestingly, we are still the only company with this open policy about disclosing microprocessor errata.

Amazingly, sales of Pentium processor–based PCs continued to rise during this crisis period, in spite of the furor on the Internet and in the press. Ironically, because of the FDIV news around the world, the Pentium processor name was everywhere and became even more firmly established in the public's mind. My mother even called me during the crisis and asked about the Pentium processor. Consumers were enamored with the multimedia capabilities of Pentium processor–based PCs and bought huge numbers of home computers during the 1994 Christmas season. Pentium processor sales rose dramatically into 1995 and soon replaced 486 processors as the most pervasive processor in all PCs.

SHORTEN DEVELOPMENT TIME

We must accelerate the product development process as we aim to get new products quickly into the marketplace. By the end of 1985, I set out to dramatically shorten and improve our product development process for microprocessors, chip sets, and microcontrollers. At this time, our development process typically took anywhere from two to four years. A number of startup companies were working on application-specific integrated circuit (ASIC) technology for developing chips much more quickly.

We decided that we must embark on an aggressive program to cut our development time by more than half. Some of the key people in the Microcomputer Group and I came up with the "52-Week Chip Program," to highlight the goal of defining a chip and putting it into production within one year. A number of people at Intel thought we were crazy, since we were taking two to four times longer than that to develop a product at the time. However, a few of us were convinced we could do it, as we saw so many areas that we could improve upon. We put forth a five-step program:

1. *Enrollment.* We got all the general managers in the Microcomputer Group to commit to the 52-week goal and to drive their respective organizations to make it happen. They participated fully in establishing the program. The benefits of the program were obvious and tantalizing: we could accelerate the delivery of newer and better products to our customers and achieve faster revenue growth. I articulated why I thought we could do this and offered specific ideas. Through the discussions, many general managers pitched in with their own ideas, and everybody got excited about making this happen. I made sure that everyone incorporated these goals and actions into their quarterly objectives and key results, so everyone had concrete milestones to reach.

2. *Indicators.* We defined indicators of progress toward the goals and posted indicator charts for products in development on walls near the development team. The charts showed detailed progress of each segment of the development process and also the status of the overall project on a daily or weekly basis. Visible indicators of the program's progress were critical to giving the team real-time feedback on how they were doing and exposing key problems. When great progress was made, public display of it gave people a wonderful sense of accomplishment. When problems surfaced, the whole team would pitch in and figure out how to solve them. Publicly displayed indicators were essential in helping the team achieve its goals.

3. *Empowerment.* We got every engineer to understand the program benefits, buy into the goals, and commit to doing whatever it took to achieve them. By holding group meetings to talk about the program, we made sure all team members understood its benefits to the company and to our customers. We typically had great discussions in these sessions. When people brought up concerns and problems, others would quickly jump in and propose creative ideas for solving them. Once the creative juices were flowing, the whole team felt empowered to contribute fresh ideas for speeding up the development process. We took concrete actions to bring in extra resources—such as better software tools and more computers—to make the engineers' jobs easier. They were delighted. We added dedicated resources to attack several key areas that were essential to the success of the program. For example, we came up with a set of standard cells, comprised of tens or hundreds of transistors that performed certain well-defined functions, that could be used over and over again. Instead of designing with individual transistors, engineers could design with predefined blocks of hundreds of transistors, making the process a lot more productive. We also developed a number of new CAD tools to speed up the design process by adding the capability to place and route these cells on a chip automatically.

4. *Reviews.* We held regular reviews of key programs to monitor progress. At these monthly and quarterly reviews teams presented highlights, lowlights, and action plans. People were always proud of their work, and a public review was a great forum to show off their results. The preparation for the review was sometimes even more important than the review itself. As the team had a chance to think through the whole program during the preparation, many insights or new ideas would emerge. The review itself was a good way for other people to see the program status, and they often shared their own ideas and experiences. In this way teams were able to learn a great deal from one another and adopt the best practices of others to improve their own work. As a result, these reviews have been very powerful in keeping our programs on track.

5. *Awards*. We presented lots of awards to teams and individuals when they achieved concrete results toward shortening the development process at the department, division, and group levels. Public recognition is one of the most powerful motivators impelling individuals and teams to do better. Everyone craves recognition by superiors and peers, and public awards are the best way to acknowledge their achievements. We also held frequent parties—ranging from ice cream socials to lunches, dinners, and special outings—to celebrate both small and big successes.

The "52-Week Chip" was a big program that involved everyone in the Microcomputer Group, and it was very successful. We improved development time by more than a factor of two in two years: from an average of 120 weeks at the end of 1985 to our goal of 52 weeks by the end of 1987. By shortening our development cycle, we were able to double the number of new products we introduced. When I presented our great results to Intel's board of directors in January 1988, I got a warm round of applause for this huge accomplishment of the whole organization. I congratulated our entire team on the success of this great effort, and everyone felt great! We held a number of celebrations for the whole team. We discovered that this five-step process was very effective in driving a large organization to achieve aggressive goals. Since then, we have employed the same management process in driving other programs within the company. In summary, the five steps are:

1. *Enrollment*. Get leaders of the organization to set aggressive yet attainable goals and to commit to achieving them.

2. *Indicators*. Post visible indicators that measure progress toward the goals.

3. *Empowerment*. Get the whole team to buy into the goals and to come up with creative solutions. Commit extra resources to help the team do the job.

4. *Reviews*. Hold regular, open, and critical reviews of the programs.

5. *Awards*. Frequently celebrate and visibly reward successes in a public forum.

DEVELOPMENT AND MANUFACTURING WORK AS A TEAM

The best way to quickly ramp a new product into production is to have product development and manufacturing functions collaborate closely from the very beginning of the product definition and design. We have learned over and over again that quality, reliability, and low manufacturing cost must be designed in from the beginning, or we have a really tough time ramping products in high volume.

In Intel's early days, we had a lot of reliability problems related to the plastic packaging of our memory products, as I mentioned earlier. We also had yield and performance problems in the early iterations of our products and had to redesign them several times to achieve the desired yield and performance levels. This took lots of extra time and effort. As a result, since the 1980s we have driven to design in quality and manufacturability. Because I had a fair amount of experience in this area, I insisted that manufacturing and reliability engineers become part of the development teams right from the beginning of their designs. By applying steady quality and manufacturing perspectives to all stages of design, the teams were able to develop high-quality products with high volume and low-cost manufacturing.

One of the keys to a successful manufacturing operation is to visibly post real-time indicators of all the important manufacturing parameters—yields, throughput time, output, and inventory—and compare the actual results with the targeted goals. In modern manufacturing operations, every process is monitored by statistical control so that corrective action can be taken immediately if a process drifts outside the control limits. This keeps inventory and rework to a minimum. Similarly, we post indicators on product development prominently on the walls of the product design areas, so everyone can see which products are doing well and which are not. When these indicators are displayed for everyone to see, corrective action can be initiated far more quickly than if they're discovered later in a routine report.

Gerry Parker runs Intel's Technology and Manufacturing Group. As head of the Microprocessor Products Group, I make sure that our two organizations work together closely as a team. We often have conflicts and issues that need to be resolved. The key is for everyone to have the same goals and a good process for resolving issues quickly. Gerry and I routinely schedule joint staff meetings where we discuss critical issues and get the teams to work together to resolve them. By role-modeling close cooperation and teamwork from the top of the organization, we send a strong message to our staffs to do the same. We often move people between the two groups to cross-pollinate ideas and experiences. Recently, two people on my staff came from the technology and manufacturing group, and Gerry's group just recruited one of my senior managers. This kind of exchange is good for both organizations.

In early 1995, as we were ramping the Pentium processor, we were totally capacity-limited and could not satisfy the market demand for these chips. We mounted a program called "Output Max" that called for many joint development and manufacturing teams around the world to achieve maximum factory output by working together on yield improvements, performance improvements, and shortening throughput time. We set very aggressive goals and motivated many joint teams from both groups to meet or beat them. The teams did a super job, producing a record volume output for 1995 and record revenues and profits for the company. We held a big celebration around the world for the two organizations, thanking the teams for their outstanding accomplishment and fantastic teamwork. This program has since become standard operating procedure at Intel, and the two teams work closely to drive maximum output everyday.

To be successful in high technology, you need to create state-of-the-art products, then be able to ship huge volumes to satisfy customer demand. For semiconductor, software, and other high-technology industries, volume is critical to achieving the high revenues needed to fund next-generation innovations. One must be relentless in finding ways to speed up product development and getting new products into the market faster. More products and more customers to buy them mean more revenues to develop even more exciting products. To achieve high volumes, you must make quality the number-one priority and design high quality, high-volume manufacturability, and low cost into the product right from the beginning. The product and manufacturing groups must work as a team to achieve the highest volumes possible.

CHAPTER SEVEN

ACHIEVE OPERATIONAL EXCELLENCE

A COMPANY ACHIEVES OPERATIONAL EXCELLENCE BY CONSISTENTLY delivering products and services to its customers as promised. Fulfilling these promises requires well-organized processes so the whole organization operates smoothly and consistently to deliver predictable outputs. Further, in the extremely competitive world of high technology, goals must be set ever higher and higher to motivate the whole organization to do better and better over time.

To achieve operational excellence, a company must have a well-articulated set of values, and management practices that guide every action and decision toward delivering consistent and predictable outputs. These serve as an internal compass that keeps the company on track, no matter what challenges it faces. Employees have to know what kind of behavior and performance the company supports and expects, so they can do their jobs and be rewarded.

Intel set its sight on achieving operational excellence right from the beginning. When the company was formed in 1968, the prevalent operational practice in the semiconductor industry was poor, with unpredictable product quality and delivery. To set Intel apart and to state its objective clearly, Intel's first advertisement conveyed a simple message, but one that clearly stated our goal: "Intel Delivers." We have been trying hard to live up to this slogan over and over again.

FIGURE 10   "INTEL DELIVERS" ADVERTISEMENT

Source: Intel

My team and I want to make our future products far better than the current ones. Intel's desire to excel, and accompanying sense of urgency, has remained as strong as when we were a startup. It is no wonder that *BYTE* magazine wrote of us, "Conventional wisdom says that Intel leads the desktop CPU market. But look at the company's development plans for the next year, and you'll see a corporation that's acting a lot more like a hyperactive start-up than a sleepy giant."[17]

INTEL CULTURE: THE HEART OF OPERATIONAL EXCELLENCE

From the outset, Intel's culture has been established and role-modeled by its founders: Gordon Moore, Bob Noyce, and Andy Grove. This culture—a set of values and behaviors everyone is encouraged to embody—has been practiced, documented, and taught at Intel for more than 25 years. Chairman Andy Grove has been the key driving force behind most of the Intel values from the founding of the company. As Craig

Barrett has taken on duties as president and executive operating officer of the company, he is playing an increasingly important role in shaping Intel's culture as we move forward.

Intel's culture revolves around six basic values, which I first listed in Chapter 3:

- Results orientation
- Discipline
- Risk-taking
- Quality
- Customer orientation
- Great place to work

I touched on results orientation, discipline, and risk-taking in Chapter 3. Here I will address how they relate to operational excellence, as well as discussing the other three values.

RESULTS ORIENTATION

Results orientation means we value aggressive goals, concrete results, and measurable outputs. A lot of meetings, e-mails, and hours of effort mean little if they produce no concrete results. One of the keys to establishing a results-oriented workplace with high output is to have concrete and quantifiable indicators for measuring outputs and results and setting aggressive goals so everyone knows exactly what they're going after.

An important management tool that helps us deliver results is a process called management by planning (MBP). Every group, department, and individual at Intel has a quarterly set of goals broken down into clear, measurable items they have to accomplish during that three-month period. All are linked to Intel's corporate strategic objectives. At the end of each quarter, individuals and groups evaluate their own performance to see what was accomplished and what wasn't. This evaluation helps us set objectives for the next quarter and keeps driving us to achieve our common goals. To keep everybody moving in the same direction, we hold quarterly business update meetings (BUMs) to which every employee is invited. At these meetings, we review the status of our business, the competitive environment, and the key accomplishments of the quarter, and then we discuss key focus areas for the next quarter. The objective of all these meetings is to ensure that everyone knows the status of the company and where it is going.

We tend to set very aggressive goals, ones that at first seem impossible to achieve. Team members work closely together to come to agreement on exactly what the goals are, taking into account market requirements and internal capabilities. An example was our goal setting for PCI chip set shipments in 1993. I maintained that we could ship one million units that year, while the general manager was targeting only 200,000 units, based on his earlier experience. I indicated my conviction that PCI would become broadly accepted by the PC industry, so that the goal of one million units was feasible. He argued that it would take time to achieve market acceptance of PCI and to build an infrastructure around the PCI business. We finally agreed on a goal of 600,000 units. The division achieved this goal by year's end, after a focused drive to get PCI accepted in the marketplace and to get new products ramping into production. It was a stretch, but the team was able to accomplish it. Everyone was elated. The next year, the same manager and his team set, on their own—and met—a goal of five million PCI chip set units, exceeding even my expectations. The team did an incredible job setting its own aggressive goals and meeting them.

One of the most powerful ways to spur everyone on to achieve a goal is to display progress indicators prominently on posters and bulletin boards. An example was our drive to ship six million Pentium processors in 1994. We posted the goal and our daily progress in a major conference room. Seeing the tangible signs of progress on a daily basis motivated people to ship more units. We achieved that ambitious goal by the end of 1994. For manufacturing, indicators are typically well understood—things like number of units produced, inventory turns, and costs. Results are also easily measured in sales: how much product has been booked and shipped, how many more deals will be closed within the next week.

Outside of manufacturing and sales, however, organizational outputs are more difficult to measure. Most companies, for example, do not measure marketing output. However, if you can't measure the output, you have no idea whether marketing is producing meaningful results. In the early days of marketing microprocessors, we came up with the innovative indicator of "design wins," described in Chapter 2, with which to measure our marketing results. A "design win" is recorded when a potential customer demonstrates its commitment to design a product using Intel microprocessors by their purchase of an Intel development system. During the "Crush" marketing campaign of the early 1980s, we watched the "design win" indicator weekly. As the number of wins rose dramatically, we knew that the campaign was working. To measure how much influence the "Intel Inside" advertising campaign had on our target audiences, we used brand awareness and end-user preference as our indicators. We collected data on these indicators by conducting focus groups with target audiences in different cities around the world. As the indicators rose, we knew that the campaign was producing the results we wanted.

In product development, one of the key indicators is time to market, measured in the number of weeks it takes a product to go from definition to production, or from the beginning of sampling to shipping one million units. One of our earliest product successes was the 486 DX2 processor, which took only 52 weeks from shipping initial samples to shipping one million production units (see Chapter 9). Since then, we have shattered that record many times.

DISCIPLINE

We value the discipline of making and meeting commitments to our external and our internal customers. When engineering makes a commitment to marketing that a new product will ship in June, they must meet this commitment so the marketing organization can plan its promotional campaigns accordingly. When marketing promised to launch a TV advertising campaign promoting the Pentium processor with MMX technology during the 1997 Super Bowl, they had to deliver on that promise to support manufacturing's plans to move product to our OEM customers and into the channels. All the pieces have to fit together perfectly if the whole program is to be successful. And this interdependence and accuracy requires disciplined planning and actions. Discipline is at the heart of operational excellence.

RISK-TAKING

Risk-taking involves embracing change, initiating change, and encouraging and rewarding individuals and teams who take informed risks. Throughout its history, Intel has taken risks, with new architectural ideas, new manufacturing processes, and new ways of marketing (covered earlier in Chapter 3). Informed risk-taking is at the heart of innovation in high technology.

QUALITY

An extraordinary commitment to quality was one of Intel's founding principles. That commitment implies a commitment to continuous improvement in everything we do. We must design in quality right from the beginning of product development and constantly set our goals higher and higher to do better over time. The conventional approach in the semiconductor industry at the time of Intel's founding in 1968 was to put nontechnical people in charge of quality assurance (QA). The function of QA was to inspect the end product to make sure the level of quality was acceptable. Unsatisfactory product was yanked and either reworked or discarded. QA people would also inspect the product line to ensure that all the operators did their jobs properly. In a way, this was like having a big police force watching people to make sure they didn't break any laws. Production workers worried only about meeting volume requirements; the responsibility for quality belonged to the QA department.

Andy Grove took a totally different approach at Intel. Right at the beginning, he put a strong technical manager—Des Fitzgerald—in charge of quality, and one of the brightest technical minds at Intel—Gerry Parker—in charge of reliability engineering. Later on, in 1974, I joined the reliability group as well. We had by far the strongest quality and reliability organization in the industry, with real technical expertise. Andy also made sure that the QA organization had the knowledge and the power to stop questionable products from shipping. One time, in the early 1980s, I wanted to put some questionable products on hold because of potential reliability problems. The general manager of memory products challenged me and told me that I was causing the company to lose revenues. I told him that shipping these products would eventually cost both our customers and us more money if we had to recall them. He did not agree, and we had a heated argument. I stuck to my position, and he eventually agreed to stop shipment until we fixed the problem. We did the right thing then and have continued to make quality a top priority in running our operations.

On the reliability side, we developed an in-depth understanding of modern silicon technology and were able to achieve reliability levels in our memory and microprocessor products that were far better than anyone else's. On the quality side, by insisting on the highest levels of quality in design and manufacturing we dramatically reduced the need for QA inspectors. We made sure that all the manufacturing and design people were responsible for the quality of their own products, instead of relying on QA for that. It was as if everyone understood that obeying the law was everyone's job, so we didn't need policemen. We were truly pioneers in this area and have maintained our high standards over the years.

CUSTOMER ORIENTATION

Being customer-oriented means listening carefully to customers and complementors. We must respond quickly to their needs and clearly communicate our intentions to them. We must deliver innovative and competitive products and services. At Intel facilities we have special parking places for our customers, but we do not provide dedicated parking spaces for our executives. Whenever a customer telephones me, I interrupt whatever I am doing to talk to that person. All Intel senior managers visit key customers on a regular basis. My staff and I meet face to face with many of our key customers at least quarterly to exchange ideas on the marketplace, our respective product lines, and how we can do better to satisfy their needs. Each session ends with a set of ARs (actions required) for both sides to take to improve our working relationships.

We set up an elaborate Vendor of Choice (VOC) program where we routinely poll key customers and ask them to rate our performance in such areas as delivery, product offering, customer service, and responsiveness in the late 80s. These performance criteria were actually determined by our customers. Based on these ratings, the executive staff each month reviews the VOC status and refines plans to support our customers better. We are so serious about this program that it is one of the criteria for determining Intel employee bonuses. When we score 90 percent on the VOC scale (meaning that 90 percent of our key customers rate us as either best or second best in their customer satisfaction ratings), everyone gets an extra day of pay. Since the beginning of the VOC program, we have reached this very tough goal three times.

Being a great place to work means that Intel is committed to providing a productive and challenging work environment for all its employees. Since the early days, new hires have been put into critical jobs right away with on-the-job training. People learn quickly from others in an open environment where problems are dealt with as soon as they surface. It has been and continues to be an incredibly stimulating environment in which to work and learn.

At Intel, people are often promoted before they are really ready. I consistently promote people based on how fast they learn rather than how much experience they have. Fast learners, when given a big task, tend to learn even faster and typically succeed even with no prior experience. For example, I promoted Pat Gelsinger to head up the critical 486 project when he was only 27 and had little management experience. I thought he was up to the job because of his vast technical knowledge and his willingness to learn everything he needed to along the way. He did very well leading the 486 team and was given a succession of more challenging assignments after that. He advanced rapidly through the ranks and was promoted to vice president of Intel's Desktop Products Group in late 1996.

Another bright engineer, Gadi Singer of the Pentium processor team, did an outstanding job creating and supporting new design tools for our design technology organization. I promoted him to run this large group, in spite of his lack of management experience. He learned very quickly and has done exceedingly well both in managing an organization with hundreds of people and in driving for a quantum leap in design tool quality. In three years, he has become the best design technology manager we've ever had.

You might say we practice nonstop on-the-job training. We have so much to do that everybody needs to contribute immediately. As a result, we provide an incredibly challenging environment for people who want to learn and advance. There are negative aspects in such an environment. People often feel stretched and overloaded. The joke is that "Intel is a great place to work, work, work . . . " It is quite true that the pace is fast and most of the jobs are very demanding. Some people thrive in this kind of environment; those who prefer a slower-paced environment will probably be happier elsewhere.

These six values constitute Intel's culture. Living them on a day-to-day basis is what enables us to deliver high output and do our jobs well.

HAVING A VISION AND MAKING IT HAPPEN

There are two key elements of Intel management systems: the strategic process (having a vision) and the operational process (making it happen). These are linked by a process of management by planning (MBP).

Our strategic process consists of two main pieces. The first is the strategic long-range planning (SLRP, pronounced "slurp") sessions, two- to three-day meetings held twice a year for the executive staff and key senior managers. At the April session, we set the company's strategic direction for the next three to five years. The November session is a midterm course check to make sure that we are still on the right track. The SLRP process begins with Andy discussing the current environment, evaluating how well we have done over the last six months in achieving our strategic objectives, and outlining his proposed changes in strategy. After extensive discussions and debates on the new strategies, we eventually come to a clear agreement on where we are going. The next step is to identify several key topics and assign each to one executive staff owner who heads a team to come back with recommended strategic direction and action plans. Again, lots of intensive discussions and debates follow before we agree what to do. After the strategic plans are thoroughly reviewed and agreed to, we publish our Corporate Strategic Objectives (CSO) on big posters that go on company walls for everyone to see. The second piece of the strategic process is the group strategic review, a two-hour discussion held each month between each of Intel's business groups and the executive office to discuss current key strategic topics for the group (for example, how should we address the emergence of digital TV?). In these sessions, we either follow up on topics from the SLRP sessions or address new topics.

To link the strategic process to the operational one, each August we put together a product-line business plan to turn strategic action plans into concrete product road maps. By the fourth quarter, these are translated into a yearly operating plan. On a quarterly basis, we hold Plan of Record reviews on overall profit and loss, progress on key programs, action plans, budgets, and any other operational issues. Each organization has its own quarterly strategic objectives and key results, which are consistent with and supportive of the overall corporate strategic objectives.

As a result of this detailed strategic planning process, the whole company is synchronized to move forward together. We review the progress of our objectives and key results on a quarterly basis so we know at any time how well we are doing and can take corrective action when progress is slower than planned. Another key piece of the operational management process is the monthly group operational review. In these sessions, each group conducts a thorough review of an important topic (such as the status of the Pentium II processor ramp) with the executive staff and other interested parties. This activity corresponds with the group strategic review on the strategic side.

The essence of Intel's management system is the close linkage of the strategic and operational processes. We believe strongly that strategic direction must be translated to concrete actions with measurable results. We are not interested in theoretical strategic ideas that lead nowhere.

OPERATIONAL MANAGEMENT

How does Intel achieve operational excellence within the MBP system and Intel culture? Key operational tools at Intel are constructive confrontation, performance management, and participatory decision-making.

In order to produce high output and achieve the desired key results, it is critical that problems are discovered and resolved quickly. It is totally unacceptable to hide problems or hope that they will go away—they won't. A hallmark of Intel is that everybody openly confronts problems and quickly gets relevant parties involved to solve them. People in my organization routinely tell me about problems they're facing, in addition to progress they're enjoying. They also present their ideas for solving these problems. In any problem-solving process, there will be disagreements and arguments. These are valuable because they spur us to discuss all angles of a problem and not miss anything. We also encourage employees to say when they disagree with someone else's idea or proposal, whether it comes from a peer, a subordinate, or a boss. This practice is essential, as senior management must hear all points of view before they can make the right decisions.

One example was the thorny issue of whether or not to remove the cache from the 386 in 1984. I wanted to leave it in, as it would improve performance. However, several people told me that they disagreed with my view. They thought it was far better to remove the cache so the project would finish on time. If the schedule were delayed, we would miss a critical market window. I finally accepted their view and agreed to take the cache out of the chip. In retrospect, it was absolutely the right decision. This course of action was possible only because people felt free to state their disagreement with a manager's view. It is perfectly OK to say, "I don't agree with your explanation of the problem, as the following data contradict it." It allows new data and new ideas to be brought into the picture.

Constructive confrontation is about criticizing issues, not individuals. It is inappropriate to drift into a personal attack: "You are totally wrong. I don't believe you." Instead, one can say, "I disagree with your proposal and here are the reasons why. . . . " The objective is to positively confront a problem, a conclusion, or a proposed plan, but not to attack the individual who came up with it. Often, there is a fine line between the two, and it is really important for people to practice constructive confrontation correctly. At one time, Intel had the reputation of being a place where "people yelled at each other." I think some people confused yelling about problems with yelling at each other. In order to practice constructive confrontation properly, we conduct a course on the subject and train every new employee how to practice it correctly.

PERFORMANCE MANAGEMENT

Managing the performance of employees is of utmost importance in getting high output from each individual. This, in turn, is critical to achieving high organizational output. We hold annual performance reviews for every employee, where a supervisor sits down with the subordinate and talks about his or her accomplishments, strengths, and areas for improvement. These are typically two-way conversations, so employees leave with a clear picture of what they did well and what they need to work on to improve. When we write performance reviews, we solicit input from an individual's subordinates, peers, and supervisor, so we get a 360-degree view. Salary increases and stock option grants are based on performance, not seniority.

I give performance feedback to my staff informally throughout the year, rather than wait for the annual reviews. People need to know what they are doing well and what they are not doing well so they can immediately take actions to improve. I believe that, when I sit down to give a performance review, there should be no surprises for that individual. The review is a summary of what should have been discussed with the employee over the course of the previous year. I also ask my staff to write a review of me, so I hear directly from them on how I can do a better job. The key to performance management is to give constructive feedback and coaching on an ongoing basis, so that performance problems can be solved quickly. Again, because of the importance of performance management, we have classes that teach managers how to do a great job monitoring staff performance.

PARTICIPATORY DECISION-MAKING

In the high-technology business, we are faced with tough decisions all the time, from technical to business to strategic issues. Each company makes decisions differently. "One-man" companies make decisions by edict. Many Japanese and U.S. companies make decisions by consensus: discussions go on until all key team members agree with the decision. Intel's decision-making process is neither dictatorial nor consensual. We call it "participatory."

Let's take the real-life example of deciding whether or not to include additional test modes in the Pentium Pro processor bus. The first step is to state clearly the decision we need to make and when we need it. In this case, the decision was whether to add four more test modes to the Pentium Pro processor bus. We had to make the decision within two weeks, or the production schedule would be severely impacted. Step two is to decide who will make the final decision (in this case, the division manager) and who needs to ratify the decision (in this case, me). Step three is to name a leader for the decision-making team. This person's job is to manage all the people involved to come up with a set of pros, cons, alternatives, and a recommendation. Finally, a decision meeting is held, with the decision maker present to make the decision. The leader presents the various alternatives, the pros and the cons, and the team's recommended decision.

In the case of the Pentium Pro processor bus, the tradeoffs were tough: the additional test modes would greatly simplify diagnosis and production testing, but the product schedule would slip by about four weeks. We had the decision meeting, where we heard strong and heated arguments from both sides. During the discussion, someone suggested implementing two of the four proposed test modes. The new information that he presented was that the two test modes would deliver 90 percent of the benefits while containing the schedule slip to just one week. From there, the decision was simple: the general manager decided to implement the two most important test modes and suffer only a slight schedule delay. I ratified the decision, and the team moved on. Many key people had participated in the discussion and in the decision process, and everyone was satisfied with the outcome. Because everyone supported the decision, implementation was easy.

A participatory decision-making process is far superior to a dictatorial style, as many people within the organization who possess much deeper knowledge than the leader are able to contribute ideas and solutions. In the high-technology business, senior managers tend to have lots of experience and broad-based knowledge, but team members working close to specific problems know a lot more about the topic at hand than the managers. It is critical that their views are heard, so that the team can arrive at a decision with the entire group's intelligence taken into account.

Participatory decision-making takes less time than consensual decision making, because it forces the decision to be made in a single meeting. Relevant parties have the opportunity to discuss the problem thoroughly and propose solutions. But there is a definitive deadline: the decision-making meeting. At times, none of the alternatives sounds very good, but the decision maker has to make a decision and get the team moving. It is much better to make a decision and move on than to become immobilized by indecision.

The decision-making process is one of the toughest we have to manage. We often have too many or too few people involved, and not everyone understands the problem statement or the boundary conditions clearly. To improve this situation, we developed a course on how to manage the participatory decision-making process; it is one of the most popular classes at Intel.

IQA: THE RACE TO DO BETTER AND BETTER

The standards for operational excellence in the high-technology business never stand still. In the 1980s, semiconductor yields in the 60 percent range were considered good, but today we must achieve yields of greater than 90 percent to be competitive. Inventory turns at four times were considered acceptable ten years ago; in today's PC business, they must be at least 40 times. DPM (defects per million) levels of 2,000 were considered good in the 1980s, but today everybody demands 200 DPM. Therefore, constant improvements in operational process are imperative in order to stay competitive year after year.

In Japan, the most prestigious award for operational excellence is the Deming Prize on Quality. It was named after American quality guru W. Edwards Deming, who introduced the quality concept to Japan and set off the dramatic improvements made by Japanese companies since World War II. Companies work for years on their operating processes in order to apply for the award. Winning the Deming award in Japan is like winning a Nobel Prize. In the United States, a similar award, the Malcolm Baldrige Award, was launched in the 1980s, but it never achieved the prestige that the Deming award has in Japan.

To motivate our whole organization to constantly improve in operational excellence, Craig Barrett initiated the Intel Quality Award (IQA) in 1991. The application process was patterned after the Baldrige Award, but the chief criterion for winning was performance according to Intel cultural values. This tied operational excellence to continuous improvement and strengthened our practice of Intel's values. In the beginning, many of the manufacturing operations applied for and won the Intel Quality Awards. Each applicant demonstrated concrete examples of the management process to achieve consistently improving product delivery as evidence of its performance with "results orientation."

In 1993, we initiated a comprehensive improvement process across the whole Microprocessor Products Group. By 1996, two of the divisions, the Microprocessor Division 6, responsible for the Pentium II processors and future processors, and the Design Technology Group, responsible for delivering design tools and methodologies, had progressed so well that they both applied for the IQA. Both had made dramatic improvements in how they operated, and I was really proud of them. The Microprocessor Division 6 won the award that year, and it was an incredible high for the whole organization.

We decided in 1996 that the whole Microprocessor Products Group—with six sites and more than 4,500 people—would apply for the 1997 IQA. This was a first, as most organizations applying were much smaller, typically a few hundred people. However, we felt that the whole group had made tremendous progress and we wanted to use the application process as a motivator to encourage everyone to do even better. We submitted our application in August 1997 and I, along with my team, made a presentation to the panel of IQA judges, showing how we had improved every part of our operations, with products coming out faster, better, cheaper, and more consistently. Three weeks later, when the news spread across the different sites that we had won the IQA award, everybody cheered. We held formal celebrations for the whole team in December 1997. But we were determined that this would be just the beginning. Next year and the year after, we would do even better! The best was yet to come.

In high technology, as in most businesses, operational results determine whether or not a company is successful. Operational excellence is achieved by having a distinct culture, a well-articulated set of values, and sound management practices. It is not enough to have a few good years. The organization must strive for constant improvement over many years and deliver consistently improving outputs for its customers. At Intel, our distinctive culture, a well-articulated set of management practices, and the internal Intel Quality Award have kept us at the forefront of operational excellence.

CHAPTER EIGHT

MAKE THE RIGHT STRATEGIC TRANSITIONS

IN THE PREVIOUS CHAPTERS, I HAVE DISCUSSED SOME OF THE KEY management principles and practices of the high-technology business, using real-life examples from Intel. The next five chapters give additional examples of these principles in action, detailing the development of our major microprocessors, from the very successful 286 for the IBM PC-AT to our latest Pentium II processor.

Let us go back to 1984. IBM's PC-AT became the de facto PC standard and was shipping in high volume. The PC clone market was just getting going and growing fast. Intel, as the key supplier of the 286 chips for IBM and the rest of the PC companies, was well positioned in the microprocessor business, while our memory business was losing ground. The demand for 286 processors was very high, and we had the enviable problem of struggling to increase production to meet demand. However, anyone who thinks that Intel had smooth sailing in the microprocessor business from 1984 to our position today would be very wrong. Between 1984 and 1989, Intel, IBM, and Compaq all faced critical strategic issues that took them in different directions. Hopefully, the many lessons learned making these strategic transitions have made us all a lot smarter.

DRIVE THE MICROPROCESSOR STRATEGY

By early 1984, I was very interested in moving into the microprocessor area. Andy Grove suggested that I talk to Dave House, Intel's general manager of the microprocessor business. Dave suggested that I take over the strategic staff role in driving product line planning and business development, which meant working closely with him. I started the new job as Director of Strategic Staff with great anticipation in April 1984.

CHART OUR COURSE

The first thing I did on this new job was to learn about the microprocessor business and get to know my partner. Dave had joined Intel in 1974 and had been deeply involved in microprocessor marketing, as well as in the microprocessor development systems business, since 1978. At a dinner meeting during which we discussed a wide range of subjects, Dave made it clear that he wanted to build Intel's microprocessor operation into a long-lasting business with generation after generation of industry-leading products. That was exactly what I wanted, too. Intel had an exceptionally strong technical sales and applications force for microprocessors. The "complete product" as delivered by the Crush campaign was very convincing. However, Intel's microprocessor product line was spread across too many markets, from embedded control to microcomputers. It did not have a sharp focus in any one area. The system and software strategy was rather poor, as evidenced by the incompatibility of Intel's development system with the rest of the CP/M world. We were both confident that we could make significant improvements by focusing on developing compelling products for the emerging microcomputer arena. In fact, we laid out an action plan and divided up our tasks. Dave would concentrate on the "survive" side of the business. As 1984 was a tough year financially for Intel, Dave would focus on managing the day-to-day business and working closely with major customers. I would focus on the "thrive" side of the business: getting our strategy and product line in great shape so that we could thrive over the long term. This division of labor worked beautifully for seven years. Though my title changed from Director of Strategic Staff to co-General Manager, with Dave managing the microprocessors, our working relationship stayed mostly unchanged.

FORKS IN THE ROAD

On the microprocessor side, Intel faced a critical transition in moving from the 16-bit 286 to the next-generation 32-bit microprocessor. The fact that we were leading in the 16-bit arena was no guarantee that we would succeed in the 32-bit world. To complicate matters, we had two separate and competing 32-bit projects underway—the 432 project in Portland, Oregon, and the 386 project in Santa Clara, California. Which one should we pick? We knew that our success in the 32-bit arena was critical, as the 32-bit microprocessor was expected to rival and surpass mainframe performance and allow us to enter the mainstream in the computing world.

The 432 project had started in 1975 when several people came up with a new architecture to handle big computing tasks that the 8080 architecture might not be able to handle. There were raging debates within the company about whether we should undertake a brand-new architecture or extend the 8080 architecture. Gordon Moore, then Intel CEO, finally decided that we should undertake a new architecture and fully fund the 432 project. He saw the 432 as a way to make Intel's microprocessor architecture truly world-class. The 432 development team put in a huge number of advanced features such as objects, redundancy, and fast bus that turned out to be far ahead of their time. The chip became very complex and big. As a result, its performance was poor. Furthermore, there was little software for this brand-new architecture. When the 432 processor was introduced in 1981, the world's attention had been captured by the immensely successful IBM PC with Intel's 8088, which became the most important microprocessor. Few people were interested in the 432. A few years later, when

IBM adopted the Intel 286 for its next major PC product, the PC-AT, industry momentum went solidly in the Intel X86 architecture direction. So the obvious question became, what would be Intel's 32-bit solution? Should we come out with a 32-bit product that was a follow-on to the 286 or should we stick with the 432? Intel had bet on a new architecture—the 432—but it had been rejected by the marketplace.

Motorola soon introduced its 32-bit 68000 processor and was marketing it aggressively. We were behind! We decided that we must start a crash program to build a 32-bit processor that would provide a smooth extension from the 286 and that paralleled the 432. There were three key design criteria: it must be 100 percent software compatible with the 8088/8086 and the 286 so that all the current software would run unchanged; it must have a world-class 32-bit architecture to run future 32-bit software well; and it must be introduced quickly so that we could regain the lead. That was a tall order. Intel architect John Crawford was tapped to come up with the architecture of the chip, and Gene Hill, who had led the 286 team, was put in charge of the design team. In 1984, the 386 was in heavy development, with people working around the clock to beat the schedule. We should have made a clear strategic transition from the 432 to the 386 and put all our resources into the 386 to ensure its success. Unfortunately, we did not. The 432 program was hanging on but languishing. There was tremendous north-south competition between the 432 team in Portland and the 386 team in Santa Clara and little cooperation between the two.

Furthermore, a major problem was surfacing for our products—a lack of 32-bit software to take advantage of the new chips. In contrast, Apple, in January 1984, had just introduced an innovative personal computer, the Macintosh, with an easy-to-use graphical user interface (GUI) for the Mac operating system and a mouse for pointing and clicking. The Mac was based on our competitor Motorola's 68000 chip. In contrast to earlier personal computers that offered only text on the screen and only a keyboard for an input device, the GUI allowed the Macintosh to display user-friendly graphics like file folders and other symbols resembling items on a desktop. The GUI and the mouse were pioneered in Xerox's Palo Alto research center, and Apple took a giant step forward by delivering an easy-to-use computer with these innovative features. As a result, the Mac became a very popular PC. A few years later, Microsoft delivered the GUI on its Windows operating system as well.

To compound our problem of being late with a 32-bit processor, we faced severe competition for our 8- and 16-bit product line. NEC was gaining market segment share against us with their version of the 8080. Other companies such as AMD and Siemens were also competing against us with "second source" versions of the 8080 and 8086. It was not a pretty picture. By way of explanation, due to spotty delivery and the poor quality of early semiconductor suppliers, customers demanded that each high-volume processor have several "second source" suppliers who would produce the same product under license from the originator. The purpose was to provide an uninterrupted supply of chips so customer production would not be impacted. As a result, we were forced to license a number of companies to compete with us with their second-source 8080, 8088, and 80286 processors.

Faced with all these critical issues, we had to move quickly. One of the key strategic questions we faced was what to do about the 432. We really did not need two 32-bit architectures. Some of us thought that the project should be terminated. However, others believed that we needed to take advantage of the 432 technology to move into next-generation systems with fault-tolerant capabilities. Siemens was interested in collaborating with us in this area and offered to put up significant development money to develop a system based on the 432 technology with us. We had a decision-making meeting with Gordon Moore and Andy Grove in 1985 about what to do with the 432 project, and both sides argued their case. It was finally decided that we would use the 432 team and technology to build a fault-tolerant computer system with Siemens. Intel would have rights to offer the resulting new processor to other customers. Some of us disagreed, but we supported the decision after it was made, in keeping with a key tenet of Intel's culture known as "disagree and commit." The joint project with Siemens was subsequently known as BIIN. Unfortunately, the BIIN chips and systems were complex and slow. The software project was very big and fell behind schedule. We eventually closed down the project. It was a very painful lesson for us.

On the other side of Intel's business—semiconductor memories—the situation was actually worse than the 432 situation in 1984. The Japanese companies were gaining more and more market segment share in memories, and we were losing badly. Intel's memory revenues dropped below microprocessor revenues for the first time in 1982. By 1984, memory revenues had dropped to only 20 percent of Intel's total. As Intel had invented semiconductor memory, we had strong emotional ties to it and were spending most of our R&D dollars and factory capacity on it. By contrast, our investment in microprocessors was relatively small. In an interesting twist, almost 40 percent of Intel's revenues and 100 percent of our corporate profits in 1984 came from microprocessors, but we were investing more than 80 percent of our corporate R&D in memories! This was clearly a "strategic dissonance,"[18] where our strategy and investments were completely out of line with reality. Andy recognized this and initiated many internal discussions on the possibility of getting out of the memory business. This was a very difficult option for us to swallow: admitting defeat on something that the corporation had created and was founded on. It was also clear that we had to do something fast, as staying the course would be disastrous. We had two choices: continue to split our attention between the memory and microprocessor businesses or make the strategic transition to focus solely on microprocessors. Which way should we go?

MAKE THE 386 HAPPEN

As Intel was facing this major strategic decision, our task in the micro-processor group was simple: make the 386 happen! With a great 32-bit microprocessor, we would firmly establish our leading position in micro-processors and leapfrog over our competition. There was no alternative. We had three "musts": 100 percent software compatibility with Intel's installed base, a world-class 32-bit architecture, and a fast time to mar-ket. John Crawford, a bright architect who works well with people, led the architectural work on the 386. He and his team came up with a very clever idea to provide software compatibility while offering a world-class 32-bit product. He proposed that we include three different modes in the chip: a real mode, a protected mode, and a 32-bit mode. The real mode ran 16-bit applications like an 8088/86, the protected mode ran software that took advantage of the 286 memory management features, and a new 32-bit mode offered new world-class capabilities for 32-bit computing. Even though it was an extension of the 286 architecture, the 386 represented a major breakthrough. Innovation of this magni-tude is only able to surface and get implemented quickly in an open en-vironment such as Intel's.

SIMPLIFY THE PRODUCT

After the 386 architecture work was completed, the next task was to finish the chip development quickly and get the product into the marketplace. There were two major technical issues to be resolved. The first was the complexity of the bus—the connection between the microprocessor and the outside world. To be synergistic with the 432 (which was still alive at the time), the 386 processor adopted its advanced bus, which was very complex. A shared bus would facili-tate building systems incorporating both the 386 and the 432, as the support chips could be the same. This would offer flexibility to our customers. However, since the 432 was not well accepted in the mar-ketplace, there was little business reason to have the same bus on both the 386 and 432.

As the 386 schedule was getting tight, the team proposed changing the bus to a simpler one, much closer to the 286 bus. This was a rational option, but the 432 team did not like the idea, as it seemed to be a slap in the face of the team who developed the advanced bus. Emotions ran high. We had several sessions arguing about it. Finally, reason prevailed, and the simpler bus was adopted. It was a tough decision for some to swallow, but it was the right one. The full discussion and participatory decision-making process really worked.

The second big issue was whether or not to include a first-level cache memory on the 386. Cache memory had been used in mainframe computers to store recently used data and instructions so the processor could operate on them quickly. Including a first-level cache on the 386 microprocessor was a revolutionary idea, and it would really speed up the performance. This, of course, would be a big leg up for the 386. The only problem was that as the project proceeded, the task of including it was getting more and more complex. Forcing it in would make the chip bigger and cause the schedule to slip. Neither was desirable. I was very reluctant to remove the cache, as it would provide a significant performance boost to the 386. Again, we had a full discussion with all viewpoints expressed. We finally agreed to remove the cache, as schedule and chip size were deemed more important than the resulting performance boost. Without the cache, the 386 die size would be smaller, which gave us lower cost and higher volume. With these simplifications, we were able to complete the 386 several months ahead of schedule! Once again, our constructive confrontation culture helped us to focus on the issue and come up with the right solution.

There were several other major challenges in building this new chip. One of them was how to quickly and efficiently pack 275,000 transistors on a chip. Today that would be child's play, as we are designing chips with up to 100 million transistors! But in 1984 no one had ever designed a chip of that complexity. Doing it by hand would be too slow and error-prone, and we knew from Moore's Law that we must push the technology frontier to move ahead. We encouraged the computer-aided design (CAD) team to come up with some automated tools to speed up the design process. Manfred Wiezel, who had just come to Intel from Bell Labs, developed some very sophisticated tools that allowed us to computerize the most tedious parts of placing and routing transistors and interconnects. These techniques were used successfully on the 386 and made the chip design complete much faster. Wiezel was a star CAD developer who went on to become a senior manager in the Pentium Pro processor design team and, later, the lead manager on our next chip.

Another big challenge was figuring out how to test the processor to ensure that all 275,000 transistors were hooked up correctly. The testing was becoming a very complex task. We came up with a number of new ideas, such as a built-in self-test, to make testing easier. In fact, because test quality was one of the major contributors to product quality, we had several people in the quality and reliability organization looking into implementing these techniques in the 386 in 1983. One of the key drivers for this was Pat Gelsinger, who subsequently led the 486 processor and other chip developments. As a result of his efforts, we were able to achieve exceptionally high quality in the 386 product through efficient testing.

A WHOLE PROGRAM, NOT JUST A CHIP

An important consideration I mentioned earlier was the need to have key software available upon introduction of the 386. Microsoft's MS-DOS* would automatically run on the 386, and we worked closely with Microsoft to ensure that DOS would not only run but run really well on our new chip. Because DOS was a 16-bit operating system, we got several small software companies to develop add-on products to take advantage of the 386's 32-bit features. UNIX* was gaining popularity as an operating system for

*Trademark

workstations and servers, and we wanted to make the 386 a good product for these important markets, too.

Richard Wirt, an Intel software expert, led the effort to ensure that we would have the best-performing UNIX and DOS operating systems for the 386 when it was introduced. Richard quickly structured a joint effort with AT&T, which owned the UNIX system at the time, to port UNIX to the 386 processor. He also built and delivered a number of early 386-based systems for software developers to use to design applications for the 386. Through his team's efforts, we were able to have the latest operating systems and key applications available when the 386 was introduced. A few years after its introduction, the 386 processor became very popular running the UNIX operating system in workstations and servers. The Santa Cruz Operation had a version of UNIX running on the 386 that became the multiuser market leader. By 1989, there were more UNIX systems running on the 386 than on any other processor. Our UNIX investments paid off well and expanded the reach of the 386 beyond the PC market alone.

Our earlier microprocessor experience taught us that there was far more to the success of the 386 than developing a first-rate chip. We had to deliver the total product: support chips, software tools, software development systems, and technical support. We needed to put together a complete marketing plan, including product positioning, promotions, and design wins programs. To make sure everything worked together, we created the position of program manager, with one person orchestrating all the pieces of the puzzle and making sure the whole thing fit together. We recruited Bruce Burkhardt from our field application engineering organization to be the 386 program manager. His technical expertise gave him a good understanding of customer and application issues. His role was to act like a major customer, to ensure that the entire 386 program was complete and that we were, in fact, delivering all the pieces of the total product. The program management idea had been used in other large projects, but the first time we applied it to our microprocessor products was in 1984. Bruce was a determined

FIGURE 11   THE 386 MICROPROCESSOR

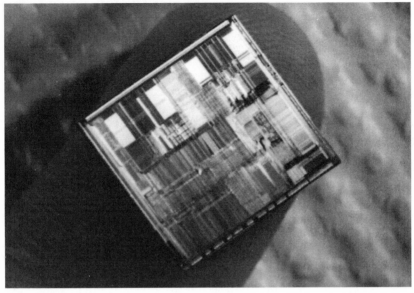

Source: Intel

guy who drove hard to make sure that all the pieces were in place. He uncovered problems that the team had overlooked and persistently drove them to resolution. Through his efforts, all the pieces of the 386 puzzle came together, and the overall program was very successful. Since then, the program management concept has been used extensively at Intel on many complex programs.

STRATEGIC TRANSITION OF A LIFETIME

By 1985, the 386 program was in pretty good shape. The chip development was speeding along quickly. To everybody's amazement, the design was completed right after the July 4th holiday, as the needed computing resources were free to run the final full-chip verification. We were two months ahead of schedule. The decision to simplify the chip by using a simpler bus and removing the cache certainly helped, as did using the latest CAD tools, which reduced the tedious manual work.

Several members of the team hand-carried the first silicon off the production line and into the laboratory to be tested. It was amazing: the chip worked the first time running Microsoft Flight Simulator, the key program used for testing functionality at the time. That was unthinkable—all 275,000 transistors worked on the first try! Everyone was ecstatic, especially me. We had been determined to make the 386 successful, as its success was a necessity for Intel to thrive in the microprocessor business. The first step was to have a great product, and we got it! In October of 1985, we introduced our new 32-bit 386 processor worldwide. We felt like proud parents of a new baby.

In parallel to this, Andy and Gordon had finally made the decision to get Intel out of the memory business and focus all our energy on microprocessors. Intel announced its exit from the memory business at about the same time we introduced the 386. This was a colossal decision for the company and the strategic transition of a lifetime. We finally overcame the emotional burden of letting go of a failing business that we had invented and focused all our energy on the business we would build our future on. It was tough. It was gut wrenching. But it was right.

We redirected a huge amount of organizational resources from memories to microprocessors. We closed many unneeded plants and redirected others from producing memories to microprocessors. We held many sessions within the company to make everyone understand why we were making this momentous transition, because we needed every employee's support. Within a short time, the whole company was marching toward the new goal—to be the world's top microprocessor company. However, the next couple of years, 1985 and 1986, were very difficult ones for Intel. As we went through this major redirection, our revenues dropped from $1.6 billion in 1984 to $1.2 billion in 1986. We suffered a huge loss of $250 million in 1986. It was a really painful period.

WHO WOULD LEAD WITH A 386 PC?

The 386 processor was a tremendous accomplishment for Intel. It was our first processor using the new CMOS[19] technology, which made the chip run faster and consume less power. It operated more than three times faster than the old 286, and met the three "musts" that I mentioned earlier: it offered 100 percent software compatibility and a world-class 32-bit architecture, and it had a timely introduction. It was a serious contender for the lead in the 32-bit microprocessor market.

However, our biggest customer didn't see it that way. IBM, the inventor of the PC, had been our major microprocessor customer from the 8088 to the 286. We were naturally eager for them to build a PC based on the 386. During the development of the 386, IBM had remained cool, skeptical that we could pull off the program. We thought that with real working silicon in hand, IBM would embrace the chip and get going on developing a 386 processor–based PC. But they did not. We were surprised and puzzled. We visited them many times and urged them to take advantage of this exciting new product. But they continued to say that all they wanted was a fast 286 and that there was no need for a 386 because there was no 32-bit software.

Dave House came up with a simple message: the fastest way to a fast 286 was a 386. The 386 was not only faster than the fastest 286, but it would also run future 32-bit software as it became available. It was the beginning of a new generation. But IBM still did not buy it and kept saying that all they needed was the 286. By the end of 1986, a year after our 386 was introduced, they still did not have an engineering team on a 386-based PC. This was very frustrating and alarming for us, as IBM was not only our biggest customer but the major trendsetter in the PC industry.

We later found out that IBM had an internal team attempting to reverse-engineer the 286, which they hoped to manufacture in their own factories. Moreover, they were also developing a proprietary 16-bit operating system called OS/2 that they intended to run on this "IBM 286." In their minds, 32-bit power belonged to mainframes, which they owned and wanted to protect. They wanted a proprietary 16-bit PC that would basically serve as an intelligent terminal linked to their mainframes. We finally understood the reason for IBM's coolness toward the 386. Soon after, their project to reverse-engineer the 286 failed. Several years later they finally embraced the 386.

Fortunately for Intel, several other PC companies were very excited about the 386. The first was Compaq. This company had made a name for itself by building compact PC products with better graphics capabilities than IBM but with 100 percent compatibility. Compaq's 286 clone was very popular. The company was small then, and its president, Rod Canion, and engineering managers Gary Stimac and Hugh Barnes were working very closely with us. They really liked the 386 and decided to design a 386-based PC in parallel with our developing the chip. Two other companies, ALR and Acer, were also aggressive in the 386-based PC area. Both were among the first wave of companies to bring 386-based PCs to market. In September 1986, Compaq introduced the first 386-based PC, the Compac Deskpro. Others followed soon after. We were excited to see the 386-based PCs from Compaq, Acer, and ALR, but we were nervous about IBM's absence. IBM was the trendsetter. If they endorsed something, it automatically became accepted by the industry. If they didn't, it would be very difficult to get a market standard established. We were afraid that without IBM, the 386 would not be accepted in the marketplace. In fact, the scariest part was that as late as December of 1986 we had 386 processors in inventory, with demand less than supply. The holiday season of 1986 was a very uncomfortable one. We had built the best product we knew how to build. We were providing the total product, from complete support chips to software development systems and tools. Our marketing programs were in place. We had made the momentous transition from memory company to microprocessor company. But where were the orders?

Fortunately, people bought lots of 386-based PCs during the December holiday season. By January 1987, huge orders for the 386 started flooding in. We faced the wonderful problem of ramping up production to maximum speed to supply the demand. It soon became clear that the 386 was the huge success we had all hoped and prayed for. It quickly became the volume leader in 32-bit microprocessors. This was also a historic moment for the industry—the first time that a new direction was set without IBM. Compaq and others jumped on the 386 opportunity and never looked back. Compaq is now the largest PC manufacturer in the world. IBM eventually adopted the 386 much later but lost the PC technology leadership role, as it did not lead with the latest chip technology.

Intel made the most crucial strategic decision of its corporate life in 1985: to focus the whole company on microprocessors and get out of the memory business it had invented. It was an extremely difficult decision but the right one. The strategic transition from a memory company to a microprocessor company was painful, but it was accomplished quickly. Intel's 386 processor was a pivotal product that dramatically changed the PC market landscape. Compaq adopted the 386 and took the lead from IBM to become the leading PC company, a position it still holds today.

CHAPTER NINE

LEAPFROG TO
THE TOP

BY LATE 1987, THE 386 WAS A ROARING SUCCESS. WE HAD PULLED AHEAD of our strongest rival, Motorola's 68030, which was used by Apple in its popular Mac. We knew lots of competition was coming. Motorola was rumored to be developing a 68040; NEC in Japan was developing its V Series microprocessor, and the new RISC chips were receiving lots of attention. In the high-technology business, one must keep aggressively moving on to the next round to stay ahead of competition. There is no resting on one's laurels. We knew we had to go forward to develop our next great product, as we wanted to continue our lead in the microprocessor business.

RISC VERSUS CISC

At the University of California at Berkeley and at Stanford University, a new concept—Reduced Instruction Set Computing (RISC) for microprocessors—was being developed around late 1985 and was generating lots of excitement. The idea behind RISC processing was fairly simple: build a processor using a small number of the most often used instructions and execute them at one instruction per clock cycle. The common practice at the time employed one instruction over several clock cycles. The result was a much simpler and faster microprocessor that would be easier to design and cost less. Of course, these promises sounded very appealing.

The Complex Instruction Set Computing (CISC) style, exemplified by Motorola's 68000, Intel's 386, and Digital Equipment Corporation's VAX, employed more (and more complex) instructions. Many RISC supporters loudly proclaimed that CISC architectures would eventually run out of steam in performance because of their complexity, and the world would move completely to RISC. The big problem with switching instruction sets was that existing software wouldn't run on new RISC processors. This would be a disaster for our end-users and thus for Intel. In my mind, the product following the 386 had to be 100 percent software-compatible with the 386. The big question was how to take a giant step forward in performance without changing the instruction set.

It was widely known that IBM was designing a number of RISC chips. Sun Microsystems was doing one called SPARC (Scalable Processor Architecture), based on the research work from Berkeley. And a new startup, MIPS, was developing yet another RISC chip using research from Stanford. Intel actually had a RISC chip underway at our Israel design facility. It was code-named the N3 and was designed to be a fast numeric co-processor that would work with a main processor to handling floating-point calculations. Unfortunately, the project was an exploratory design without a clear business goal in mind. It drifted aimlessly, and the chip got bigger and more complex without the normal comprehensive reviews. The project was eventually terminated. From this and other projects, we learned over and over again that successful products begin with clear business goals in mind. Projects must also be reviewed regularly to ensure that the team is delivering what it is supposed to. If not, corrective action needs to be taken to get the program back on course.

So, what was our plan to develop the follow-on to our successful 386 while ensuring total software compatibility? A team of architects headed by John Crawford came up with the simple idea of running RISC-like instructions very quickly—while maintaining software compatibility—by running more complex instructions on an improved microarchitecture (the internal workings of a microprocessor that perform the computing functions). Because we had the newest silicon technology available, we could pack about a million transistors on this new chip, almost four times more than the 386 had. We decided to utilize the extra transistors to build the new microarchitecture. We also integrated the cache memory we had removed from the 386 chip, as well as a floating-point unit (a separate chip that performs mathematically intensive calculations), on a single piece of silicon. The resulting chip would be 100 percent binary-compatible with the 386 but would run much faster. It was an innovative way to combine the best ideas of RISC while preserving the treasured software compatibility. We were all elated with this breakthrough. We called this product the 486 processor. We needed a strong leader to manage this project aggressively, and Pat Gelsinger fit the bill perfectly. He was bright, aggressive, and worked really hard to learn and perform. Pat very quickly built a strong development team that was up and running by early 1986.

860 VERSUS 486

At the time the 486 processor was getting underway, Intel had several other microprocessors in development. The Intel/Siemens joint venture, BIIN, was developing microprocessors and systems based on the 432. We also had a skunk-works RISC project run by two bright engineers, Les Kohn and Sai-wei Fu. They had salvaged some ideas from the Israel-based N3 project to use on a new RISC chip that promised to be simple to design but would have super-fast floating-point performance, which would be very useful for scientific and graphics applications. Les Kohn was a talented but shy architect. Sai-wei Fu was an experienced designer who had worked on the 432 project. They put together a floor plan for the RISC chip and showed me the virtues of their elegant design. I was intrigued by its simplicity and potential for high performance. At the same time, I did not think we could afford another architecture. Should we kill this project or go for it with a clear business objective? I discussed this with Dave House in great detail. This chip would not be a mainstream processor like the 486, but it showed real promise as a super floating-point math co-processor for the 486. We could also learn a lot by implementing a RISC chip and seeing the positives and negatives firsthand. We finally decided to fund the project, code-named the N10 (indicating that it was a numeric processor), which we subsequently named the 860. The 860 got going in early 1986, about the same time as the 486. Was it risk-taking? Absolutely.

The 486 and 860 design teams were both located in Santa Clara, and a competition quickly arose between the two to see who would finish their chip first. Actually, it was very interesting to see a pure RISC chip, the 860, competing in implementation with a partial RISC chip, the 486. Both chips required about one million transistors, and both took about two and a half years from early definition to first silicon. The 486 team was about 15 percent larger than the 860 team. Actually, both teams learned quite a bit from one another. Some of the RISC-type microarchitecture of the 486 benefited from the 860 work, and much of the design methodology for the 860 was borrowed from the 486 and the 386. By tackling both chips, Intel was the only company that understood the details of both RISC and CISC.

By late 1988, we saw the first 860 silicon. It worked on the first try and its performance was excellent. The first silicon of the 486 was ready by early 1989, and it, too, worked the first time. The whole 486 team had been working three shifts to get the job done, and it was exciting and gratifying to see the chip work so well. In fact, the 486 team had planned to have the chip done by Christmas of 1988 but didn't make it. So the whole team worked through the holidays and celebrated Christmas in February, complete with Christmas trees in their offices.

At the same time, Motorola was working hard on its competing product, the 68040 processor, but their development fell further and further behind ours. We introduced the 486 in April 1989 with a big show: laser lights, speeches, and many operating 486-based PCs on display. Motorola actually announced the 68040 a few days before the 486, but they had no silicon or systems to show. They eventually completed the chip, but the 68040 lagged behind the 486 significantly in performance and in volume. The 486 was on its way!

THE SPARC CHALLENGE

By the end of 1988, Sun's RISC processor, SPARC, had been in production for about a year, and it outperformed the Motorola 68030 chip which Sun had been using in its workstation system at that time. Sun's original motive in creating the SPARC chip was to create a processor that was faster than the 68030 for running UNIX. They succeeded. In fact, Sun stopped using the Motorola 68000 processors altogether and replaced them with their own SPARC chips in their workstations. Motorola subsequently lost all its workstation customers and had only Apple as a volume customer. Apple later replaced the Motorola chips, too, switching to the PowerPC in 1991.

Sun became a very successful workstation and server company using its own RISC processors. Seeing the potential of the SPARC chips, Sun decided to expand into the general-purpose microprocessor business, in direct competition with Intel. Sun formulated an aggressive strategy and mounted attacks on several fronts. First, Sun touted the SPARC architecture as an open architecture (versus Motorola and Intel). Then it positioned UNIX as an open operating system (versus the proprietary operating systems such as VMS that are only available to the originating company) and used "openness" as the basis for a major marketing campaign. Sun licensed the SPARC architecture to many semiconductor companies around the world, including Fujitsu, Toshiba, LSI logic, Texas Instruments, and others, to make sure that there would be plenty of vendors to supply the chips at low prices.

Sun also formed an international SPARC users group with broad membership from many companies, to demonstrate that

SPARC was an open architecture. Next, they urged PC manufacturers to build Sun clones just like the IBM PC clones. By early 1989, they were strongly pushing their marketing messages to Taiwanese PC companies such as Acer and Tatung, urging them to build SPARC clones to replace the PC. They also put together an aggressive marketing pitch, touting the virtues of RISC and claiming that Intel's CISC architecture would soon run out of steam and lead to a dead end. They pushed UNIX as the open operating system standard, versus Microsoft's DOS/Windows. They claimed that UNIX-based PCs running on SPARC microprocessors would replace Windows-based PCs. Their strategy was clearly to position Sun's UNIX and associated applications as the key products of high value while relegating microprocessors to the status of low-cost commodities. Many of the claims sounded very appealing. However, reality turned out to be very different.

When it was all unfolded, Sun's SPARC offensive loomed as a major strategic threat to Intel. We were under tremendous pressure from Sun beginning in 1988. The press was fanning the hype that RISC was better than CISC, and many opinion leaders predicted that SPARC would replace the Intel architecture, just as Intel's architecture had replaced Motorola's 68000.

In fact, Intel had a very strong product portfolio in 1989: we not only had a high-performance 486 that was 100 percent compatible with all existing PC software, but also the blazingly fast, RISC-based 860. The question was, how should we position our two products in the marketplace? Microsoft was also under attack from Sun during this time, as Sun aimed to replace the DOS/Windows operating systems with UNIX. Microsoft's chief technologist, Nathan Myhrvold, was very excited about the 860 and was also of the opinion that RISC would someday overtake CISC. He saw the opportunity to build a RISC-based PC running the new Windows NT operating system, instead of UNIX. In fact, Microsoft built a prototype PC based on the 860 and was trying to get several PC manufacturers interested.

At Intel, there was a great deal of internal debate about RISC versus CISC. Should we use the 860 to fight the RISC threat? Should we stay the course with the 486 and keep the 860 as a co-processor? Dave House and I and many others had lots of intense discussions about this critical decision. Finally, Dave and I decided to fight Sun head on, positioning the 860 as Intel's RISC chip for the workstation and supercomputer market, rather than pursuing our original plan to position the 860 as a fast floating-point co-processor. We decided to launch the 860 in February 1989 in San Francisco with a big event. We introduced the world's first one-million-transistor chip and demonstrated its blazingly fast performance by showing real-time color computer graphics on many 860 systems. The press and the analysts were very excited about this technology-leading product, and stories on the 860 appeared everywhere.

Then reality hit. We ran into the same big problem that the other RISC companies faced: there was no software for a brand-new architecture. We had pushed hard to get the UNIX and Windows NT operating systems running on the 860 and to get a critical mass of application software in place. However, all this took time. Our task was made even more difficult because independent software vendors showed little interest in devoting their precious resources to a new processor with small volume. We also realized that the high-end workstation and supercomputer markets at the time were too small to warrant a chase with a totally separate architecture from the mainstream. We could not afford the huge investment in software infrastructure and chip development to justify a reasonable return on the 860.

The other RISC-based processors ran into exactly the same problem. For the SPARC chip, the problem was even worse. First, there were many semiconductor companies competing to supply a very small SPARC market. Realistically, none could afford the needed investments to keep development going if they were to sell only a small quantity of chips. Second, SPARC system cloners were also competing for this same small market, and they could not continue to invest with little or no return either. I went to Taiwan in 1989 and visited many of the PC companies that were considering building SPARC system clones. I presented my view that it did not make business sense to build these SPARC clones with no returns in sight. Making matters worse, Sun, while proclaiming that their UNIX was open, was not releasing its latest version of the UNIX operating system to the cloners, making them noncompetitive in the marketplace.

Third and perhaps most important, the promised RISC performance advantage turned out to be transitory, as the 486 quickly became faster and eventually surpassed SPARC's performance in 1991. The reality was that the Intel architecture had incorporated many RISC and other good architectural ideas and was able to improve in performance rapidly, as shown by the subsequent 486 DX2 and Pentium processors. Just as importantly, UNIX was not suitable for the average PC user; it was too big and too complex to be affordable by the masses.

By 1990, it became clear that Sun's assault on the PC and on Intel was totally unsuccessful. Today, the SPARC chips have basically one customer: Sun. The SPARC chip's performance has lagged behind Intel's processors since 1991. Most of the Sun cloners went out of that business, and companies like Tatung created Sun clones only to demonstrate their engineering prowess. UNIX systems had been shipping close to a million units a year, a mere 1 percent of the 100 million PCs based on the Intel architecture estimated for 1998.

Our 860 was unsuccessful for the same reasons. We had a few customers in graphics and supercomputing, but the impact and volume of the 860 were minimal. Microsoft's RISC PC went nowhere. Both Les Kohn and Sai-wei Fu left Intel, and they now work for C-Cube in Santa Clara designing MPEG chips. We at Intel put all our efforts into the 486 and its successors. Thinking back, developing the 860 technology was a good thing to do, as we learned a lot about RISC techniques and fast floating-point computing. However, introducing it as a second major computer architecture from Intel was a mistake. We should have stuck to our original intent and kept it as a super floating-point co-processor for the 486. We took a risk with the 860 and the strategy did not work. We learned a lot and moved on.

Users soon realized that Intel-architecture PCs were fast, inexpensive, had plenty of software, and were improving rapidly. Although the SPARC attack fizzled, Intel would face the RISC challenge several more times, each time with basically the same results.We had the unique experience of both defending against these RISC challengers and waging a RISC offensive ourselves with the 860. As a result, we understood both CISC and RISC technologies really well. We incorporated our learning to make our next-generation products better and better. The lesson from the RISC competition was simple: stay with the architecture that brings volume. Volume generates revenues, profits, and development resources for more new products. No volume means no business. It's that simple.

WIN WITH THE 486

THE FASTEST PROCESSOR: THE 486!

It was clear to us what we should do in the face of strong competition. We must continuously drive for higher volumes and higher performance for our products, following Moore's Law. We aggressively drove to ramp the production of 486 around the end of 1989 and devoted all our resources in Santa Clara to resolving the many production startup problems of a new product. At the same time, we knew we had to drive the 486 performance improvements. We decided to use a separate Portland, Oregon–based team, part of our technology development organization, to design a smaller 486 chip on the then-new 0.8-micron silicon technology[20] that would run faster and cooler. Remember the benefits of a new silicon technology? At the time, the 486 was operating at 25 MHz on 1.0-micron technology. We wanted the 0.8-micron version to push toward 50 MHz, two times faster. That was a very ambitious goal. In addition, we saw an opportunity to expand the role of the 486 into the PC server market by having a high-performance cache memory chip at 50 MHz to go with the processor. The task of designing a pair of high-speed processor and cache memory chips was a huge technical challenge and the Portland team was pushing both the design and the silicon technology to their limits. The Santa Clara team was improving the older 1.0-micron 486 while working closely with the Portland team on the 0.8-micron version. By late 1990, we saw early samples of the 0.8-micron chips. They performed beautifully, and some even ran much faster than our 50-MHz target—up to 90 MHz. We were delighted.

A simple idea came to us: why not show the world that the 486 could operate at 100 MHz, a performance level that no one expected? This would absolutely take the wind out of the sails of all the RISC-chip defenders, as no RISC could operate at that speed. More important, our customers would see that the 486 had lots of performance head room and they could rest assured that they would have leadership PCs based on our future processors that would run faster and better. We decided to present a technical paper at the International Solid State Circuit Conference in February 1991 telling how we achieved a 100-MHz 486 in our lab. There were many at Intel who doubted whether we could, in fact, pull off this feat, much less have it ready in time for the conference. But the Portland team really came through, and by working day and night produced a few 100-MHz parts to show that it was indeed possible. Joe Schutz, the team leader, presented the historic paper at the conference in San Francisco that February. The audience was stunned. In addition to technical people attending the conference, many analysts and press representatives heard this incredible news from Intel. They wrote many stories about how the 486 was actually outperforming SPARC! The Sun people were said to be shocked and dismayed by our 100-MHz 486 demonstration. We had just taken their performance leadership from them.

It was important for us to get ahead in the public's perception. But the real task was to get going and deliver high-performance 486 processors in volume. We were pushing to ship 50-MHz products in volume, but the schedule was slipping due to tremendously difficult technical problems. We were exploring many technology frontiers with this part. Finally, we resolved all the issues and announced the 50-MHz 486 and the cache memory in June 1991 and started shipping.

INVENT THE DX2 PROCESSOR

By the fall of 1991, we were facing serious competition from AMD. A few years earlier, AMD had put together a team in Texas to reverse-engineer our 386, coming up with a product called the AM386 that was supposed to behave just like Intel's 386. AMD had been increasing its 386 production and was beginning to take a lot of business from us. They had an easier time generating business than our RISC competitors, because AMD could supply chips to the existing healthy PC market. They did not have to generate new software or new system designs as the RISC guys had to. The competition from AMD's 386 was very worrisome to me.

Then, an unexpected event turned the situation in our favor. Microsoft introduced their new operating system, Windows 3.0, in May 1990. It employed a new graphical user interface that made the PC much easier to use, like Apple's Mac. Windows 3.0 was also capable of running multiple applications simultaneously. It became an instant success. In order to run Windows 3.0 and the associated applications well, users required more powerful PCs. As they began to flock to this new operating system, they found that 386-based systems were too slow. Almost overnight, everyone wanted a PC with a powerful 486 processor to run Windows 3.0 well. We increased our production volume of the 486 to supply the exploding demand. We were a step or two ahead of AMD, which only had a 386 to sell.

We could not stand still. We moved to drive the 486 to even higher performance. In the process, we ran into several roadblocks. First, we faced major technical challenges producing the 50-MHz

486 processors and the 50-MHz cache memory and getting them to run together. As we pushed the performance higher, it was getting increasingly difficult to push the bus to higher speeds. Second, PC designers were having major technical difficulties designing mother-boards at 50 MHz. They had to shorten the interconnects and de-sign special circuits to make 50-MHz 486-based systems work. Therefore, when we got the processor to 100 MHz, no one seemed to know how to design a 100-MHz system. We had lots of discus-sions about these tough problems. If we didn't solve these, we couldn't drive PC performance any higher.

One day, one of our strategic marketing managers, Bill Rash, came to my office and excitedly told me that he and two other fel-lows had come up with an interesting idea while talking in the cafe-teria. He said there was no reason why the internal speed of the processor and the external speed of the bus had to be the same. As soon as the words were out of his mouth, I saw how elegant the solu-tion was! The idea was simple: let's make the internal speed of the 486 run as fast as possible, so it could do high-speed computations, but have the external bus speed run at half the speed of the internal speed. This simple and innovative solution was one more example of how an open environment and a problem-solving focus enable new ideas to surface quickly.

We called this "clock doubling" because the internal clock speed of the processor is double the speed of the bus. For example, the internal speed of the chip might be 50 or 66 MHz, while the ex-ternal bus speed could be only 25 or 33 MHz. By placing the first-level cache memory inside the 486, many programs could run totally within the 486 chip without having to access the main memory through the bus. Thus, the performance would not be im-pacted with a half-speed bus. This brilliant but simple idea solved the most difficult problems facing both chip and system designers, as both were struggling to deal with the high bus frequencies. Now, a 50-MHz processor would have only 25 MHz on the bus, which would be accommodated by the 486 systems already on the market.

No engineering changes were needed to accept this new and higher-performance processor!

The next task was to figure out how to get this product designed, as all the design teams were tied up. It so happened that a team working on a microprocessor for embedded control, the 960 (a follow-on to the terminated BIIN project), in Portland, Oregon, was finishing up. Many experienced designers would soon be available. So, we decided to start up a team in Portland to do the 486 clock-doubling part, later named the 486 DX2. Pat Gelsinger, who completed the 486 design, was running a platform architecture organization in 1989 to boost graphics and platform performance. Pat had long wanted to move his family out of Santa Clara to a country-like setting more like his hometown in Pennsylvania. Portland was just such a place. When I asked him if he was willing to move to Portland to start this project, he accepted gladly.

His team's main job was to develop a 66-MHz part with a 33-MHz bus, which would put us at the leading edge in performance against RISC challengers. Pat put together a very experienced team and got going quickly. By taking full advantage of the latest silicon technology, the team was able to get the 66-MHz processor done in record time. Remember, we had achieved speeds as high as 90 MHz inside the chip. With the "clock doubling" technique, the bus only needed to be at 33 MHz, an easy task. We introduced the 66-MHz 486 DX2 in 1992, and it was an instant success for two simple reasons. PC manufacturers could command a higher price for the 66-MHz 486 DX2–based PCs because of the extra performance, and almost no engineering work was required. All they had to do was to plug the DX2 part into existing 33-MHz 486 systems.

This plug-in design led to another innovative new business for us: processor upgrades. If it was so simple for OEMs to plug in the new processors, why not offer similar plug-in processors directly to end-users? The benefits were clear: users could upgrade their systems simply by buying a higher-MHz processor and plugging it into their existing PCs. They instantaneously got a much faster system. We created an entire line of Intel OverDrive® processors which we sold directly to end-users in late 1992. That business became an instant success and got Intel into selling processors directly to end-users.

This simple clock-doubling idea revolutionized the whole microprocessor business. First, it made faster and faster processors possible without burdening the system design. Just about every processor today is either clock-doubled or clock-tripled. It also opened up a brand-new business for Intel. And it illustrates how innovation can come about: marketing and engineering people were talking about a tough problem and came up with a great solution. Bill Rash and the co-inventors of clock-doubling were given special awards for their outstanding contributions. Bill has moved on and is now directing the definition of our 64-bit processor product line.

In addition to the DX2 at the high end of the 486 line, we came up with another innovation for a low-end product. From a business perspective, we needed a lower-priced 486 to expand the market at the high-volume entry level. The team came up with a new product that we called the 486 SX, which was a 486 without the floating-

FIGURE 12   INTEL 486 DX2 PROCESSOR

Source: Intel

point unit. Many business applications did not use floating-point processing, and this version allowed us to offer a lower-cost product for entry-level systems. We introduced the 486 SX in 1991 and called the original 486 the 486 DX. At the time, many reporters and analysts criticized our strategy, calling the 486 SX a crippled 486. They were wrong, as the 486 SX generated the highest volumes of all the 486 parts for years.

THE FOUR Ps OF MARKETING

By 1992, we had the three key 486 products on the road map: the DX had been in high volume production for almost two years. The SX was introduced in early 1991 and was being received well as the entry part. The 50-MHz 486 and cache were shipping in volume to the server market, and the DX2 was well on its way. We decided that we would put all our marketing and manufacturing resources behind the 486 product line. The 486 was clearly what end-users wanted to run Windows 3.0 and associated applications well.

In driving the 486 business, we focused on the four Ps of marketing: product, price, promotion, and placement. From the product point of view, we had a complete product line: the 486 SX, 486 DX, and 486 DX2. This product road map enabled our OEM customers to offer a complete line of PCs from the entry level to the mid-range and to the high end. In addition to desktop and mobile PCs, the 486 with the fast external cache was a great combination for building PC servers with superior price/performance.

Next, we aggressively priced the whole product road map to expand the market. OEM customers wanted a full line of products, with prices to match. We had the 486 SX on the bottom, with low prices for entry-level systems; the 486 DX in the middle for mid-range systems; and the 486 DX2 at the high end for premium-priced desktops and servers. As the DX2 was the fastest of the processors, we could set a higher price, since power users were willing to pay for the extra performance. This pricing strategy worked well for our customers and for us. The low-end product provided the volume expansion, while the high-end products provided more profits for us and our customers.

Promotion was the next order of business. We mounted a major marketing campaign touting the benefits of 486-based PCs over 386-based PCs. The most obvious reason was the extra performance it provided for running Windows applications. But there was another good reason: many 486 systems were upgradable with OverDrive processors, while 386 systems were not. Armed with these clear and simple messages, our marketing organization put together promotional programs that included advertising, trade shows, and press releases and began spreading these messages.

To place these products, we worked closely with our major PC customers and helped them to ramp their 486 products in volume with us. The reactions were really interesting. Newer companies such as Dell and Acer were extremely excited. They saw the new products as an opportunity for them to gain market segment share. They rapidly designed 486-based systems and mounted aggressive marketing programs that were in synchronization with ours. In fact, Dell was one of the first PC companies to distribute PCs by mail order. They were the first mover on the 486 and dramatically gained market segment share and became a major player. On the other hand, the strategies of the two big PC leaders were very different, each toying with RISC alternatives.

THE POWERPC AND MIPS THREATS

The IBM situation was complex. On the one hand, their PC group, under new management, became very aggressive in adopting our new microprocessors. On the other hand, others at IBM were determined to use their own proprietary processors. While we were putting the finishing touches on our 486 line, IBM got Apple and Motorola interested in developing a new family of RISC processors called the PowerPC that was based on IBM's proprietary RISC technology.

Apple could use these chips in a new line of high-performance PCs, and Motorola could sell them on the open market.

IBM, Motorola, and Apple announced the three-way PowerPC alliance in July 1991, promising to deliver a family of PowerPC chips that would be faster and cheaper than ours. Here was the second major RISC threat; we were very concerned. The alliance, if successful, would benefit Motorola, which was almost out of the microprocessor business now that its 68000 family could not compete with the 486 and was being dropped by Sun, Apple, and many of their other customers. The PowerPC gave Motorola another chance to get back into the microprocessor market with IBM's and Apple's investments.

Apple had been looking for an alternative microprocessor for their PCs to replace Motorola's 68000 processor family, which was not competitive in the marketplace. Before the PowerPC alliance was formed, we were campaigning very hard for Apple to adopt our microprocessors. We showed them our 486 DX2 microprocessor as well as future products on the drawing board that would offer them the best processors for their PCs for years to come. Apple was very interested. They formed a special team to put the easy-to-use Mac operating system on a prototype Apple PC with our microprocessor. The demonstration worked nicely. We thought Apple was very close to coming our way until some key managers supporting this project left the company. Instead, Apple jumped on the PowerPC bandwagon, obviously believing the RISC performance and cost claims.

The economic benefits of the PowerPC to IBM were much less clear, other than their desire to use their own processors in their product line. They would have to manage two architectures for their PC line: the Intel architecture and the PowerPC. The investments required would be huge. Also, they did not have software to take advantage of the PowerPC in the volume PC market. Ultimately, very little came of the PowerPC alliance. Many of the PowerPC products were late and inferior in performance. The PowerPC threat eventually faded.

When we were talking to IBM's PC group about our planned move to the 486, they had just undergone major management changes. Bob Corrigan was named head of the company's PC business, and he was determined to boost IBM's PC market share. In the process, he did away with a great deal of IBM bureaucracy, even relaxing the dress code. At one meeting in Somers, New York, I met a roomful of IBM PC managers who were all wearing sweaters and open shirts, a dramatic change from the white shirt–blue suit uniform. Under Corrigan's management, IBM moved rapidly into the 486 market and did very well.

Compaq's strategy with the 486 was different again. As I indicated earlier, Compaq was the first mover in the 386 market, introducing the very first 386-based PC and became one of the fastest-growing PC companies. Unfortunately, their PC became overengineered and expensive. By 1991, Dell was aggressively taking business away from Compaq with a series of advertisements pointing out that Dell's systems were half the price of Compaq's. Dell was doing really well with that strategy, in addition to becoming the first mover on the 486. Meanwhile Compaq faced a strategic issue of whether to use a RISC chip instead of our microprocessors.

A startup company called MIPS developed another RISC processor, also called MIPS, that was based on research work at Stanford University. MIPS was aggressively trumpeting the same message SPARC and PowerPC had earlier: RISC was good and CISC was bad. They claimed that the MIPS chip would outrun and outperform chips such as Intel's 486 and eventually put Intel out of business. MIPS signed up a number of semiconductor companies, including NEC, Toshiba, and Siemens, to supply the MIPS chips cheaply, just as Sun had. Bob Miller, CEO of MIPS, was successful in getting several computer companies, such as Silicon Graphics and DEC, to join a consortium called ACE (Advanced Computing Environment) to develop PC platforms based on the MIPS chips. They even got Rod Canion, president of Compaq, interested in joining ACE to adopt the MIPS chips for their PC, instead of our chips.

This was the third major RISC-based processor threat to Intel, after SPARC and PowerPC. We were very worried. Canion met with a few of us from Intel at a hotel in Santa Clara, California, early in 1991 to tell us about Compaq's interest in ACE. We demonstrated the great performance levels of 486 products in development that were competitive with any of MIPS's claims. We urged him to take full advantage of our chips and be the first mover again with the 486, as he had with the 386. Canion felt he was already leading in the 486-based PCs but he was clearly consumed by RISC fever. A month later, we traveled to Compaq headquarters in Houston to show him concrete data that Compaq was actually way behind in the 486 market. Soon after, Eckhard Pfeiffer replaced Canion as Compaq's CEO. Pfeiffer immediately focused on the important task of cutting costs and taking advantage of the 486 volume opportunity. He also took decisive action to pull Compaq out of ACE and focus the company on one architecture: the Intel architecture. Compaq lost money in 1991 but bounced back strongly to become the PC volume leader by 1994, mostly on the strength of its 486 product line, its focus on cutting costs, and its aggressive drive to gain market segment share.

ACE faltered badly after Compaq pulled out. Each member had a different agenda. MIPS could not succeed in the microprocessor business for the same reason that SPARC and PowerPC could not: lack of software and volume. In 1992, Silicon Graphics bought MIPS and used the chips mostly for its own computers for 3D graphics applications. ACE soon faded away. SPARC's situation was similar: it was mostly used only in Sun's computers in the UNIX market. PowerPC basically had two customers: IBM and Apple. Andy Grove came up with an appropriate term for these RISC processors—MORP, which stood for "my own RISC processor." Each of these chips has been used principally by a vertically integrated computer company for their own systems. It will be interesting to see what happens to these MORPs as the parent companies face the strategic decision to continue to differentiate by developing their own microprocessors or to use merchant microprocessors like Intel's and differentiate their systems by adding value on top of the microprocessors such as applications, service, and support. Bob Miller left Silicon Graphics and started a successful workstation company called Net-Power a few years later based on our Pentium Pro processor chip.

ON TOP!

By 1992, both Compaq and IBM, along with just about every other PC manufacturer, had jumped on the 486 bandwagon, causing 486 volume to soar. The 486 ignited the PC market growth by attracting more users and creating more uses for the PC. The price became affordable, and the PC became truly powerful. The overall PC market grew from 20 million units per year in 1990 to more than 40 million units in 1991. The growth has continued and it is expected to approach 100 million units by 1998, according to several market research firms. By 1993, Intel surpassed NEC as the largest semiconductor company in the world, on the strength of the 486. Thinking about the horrible time we had in 1985, when we got out of the memory business due to the pressure from Japanese companies, it was gratifing to come back and pass them eight years later in microprocessors. It had been a very tough eight years.

There were many factors that contributed to the huge success of the 486 processor. Timing was critical. The accidental coincidence of the 486 with Windows 3.0 and Windows applications was a big factor. Development of new distribution channels such as mail order contributed greatly to the volume and reach of the PC market. Our innovative product road map and solid operational execution were also big factors in the success. We faced many challenges from our competitors, such as the RISC camp with SPARC, MIPS, and PowerPC, and imitators such as AMD. Most importantly, we focused all our resources on the four Ps of marketing: product, price, place, and promotion. We planned and developed a strong product family. We worked hard to price the products right, at the right moment, to sell the highest volumes. Promotion was critical: we articulated clearly the key reasons why people should want the 486. And we placed the entire product line into the right channels to reach the right end-user.

Coordinating the four Ps of marketing was difficult and complex. But orchestrating all these pieces was critical to the success of most new products. We did an OK job on the 386 and a much better one on the 486. The first step was to ensure that each of these activities had a clear owner. For the 486 family, I was responsible for the products, driving the creative juices to come up with the innovative ideas for the 486 and the DX2. Paul Otellini, who shared management of the Microprocessor Product Group with me at the time, was responsible for the positioning and pricing: determining the right position and right prices at the right time. Dennis Carter, vice president of marketing, was responsible for correctly promoting our products and advertising them right. Carl Everett, vice president of sales, was responsible for placement—selling the right products through the right channels.

The second critical step was to make sure that the four owners worked smoothly to collaborate on these activities. For example, as we needed to extend our broad product line to volume low-end systems, it was essential to have a low-price product like the 486 SX in place. Paul worked with me to come up with the product, which was the simplest part—it involved removing the floating point of the chip. But placing and promoting the 486 SX were more challenging. Paul took the lead and worked closely with Carl and Dennis to orchestrate the campaign that made the SX a successful high-volume product. In the case of the 486 DX2, I took the lead, as it involved major product innovations. I worked closely with the other three to launch this product and persuade customers to design the chip into their systems quickly. Paul and I worked hard to position and price these products so we would have a coherent lineup. We all collaborated with Carl to get our customers closely linked to our programs. Dennis led on crafting the right promotion programs for the DX2. I joined forces with Gerry Parker, who was in charge of technology and manufacturing, to deliver high volumes of 486 products in every flavor. We had many short conversations and e-mail exchanges to get things coordinated and moving fast. We also held regular meetings to grapple with a large number of issues like capacity planning, pricing, and positioning, and to get all the organizations moving in the same direction. We made some mistakes along the way, but our overall teamwork and coordination worked well in our drive to bring the new 486 product into the marketplace. We learned a lot from this experience and tried to apply the essence of teamwork and constant communications to our other product launches.

After we introduced the 386, many competitors were on our heels, wanting to take business away from us. There was no time to rest on our laurels; we had to move quickly to invent the next new product. Intel not only expects but welcomes strong competition. The trick is to outrun and out-execute them, finishing faster and better. We focused on delivering volume product. In the high-technology business, volume is the key to profits which fund development of more new products. Lack of volume spelled trouble for the RISC processors. We focused on excellent execution of the four Ps of marketing—product, pricing, promotion, and placement—in driving the 486 processor into the marketplace. We orchestrated the whole team to move in the same direction with constant communications and focus.

CHAPTER TEN

OBSOLETE OUR
OWN PRODUCTS

WE LEARNED EARLY ON THAT GIVEN THE PACE OF TECHNOLOGICAL advances predicted by Moore's Law, we must continue to develop better and better products to obsolete our existing products, or someone else will do that for us and leave us behind. The last chapter described how the development of a whole family of 486 products obsoleted our own 386 processor, which had obsoleted our 286 earlier. The real benefactors of all these new and better offerings are consumers, who have available to them more and better digital products to satisfy their every need. What's next after the 486?

PENTIUM® PROCESSOR TO OBSOLETE 486

After the 486 was launched at the end of 1989, we began to think about coming up with a new blockbuster product to obsolete it. We had lots of very strong competition. The computing world was still enamored with the RISC promise of a simpler and faster processor that was cheap to design and build. It turned out that these RISC chips became much more complex as they entered the real world of computing. At the same time, their actual performance and promised cost benefits were seldom realized. Also, the investments needed to keep them competitive became equally enormous. We found ourselves in the same boat with the 860, and had to discontinue development in 1991 because we could not afford the big investments needed to keep that architecture competitive. Nevertheless, the RISC threat continued to confront us, as these challengers kept pushing to achieve higher and higher performance with the hope of capturing a piece of the volume PC market. At the same time, the companies such as AMD and Cyrix that had built 386 processor imitators began to come out with their 486 imitations.

By early 1990, when our engineers were coming off the 486 development team, we moved quickly to develop our next-generation product, code-named P5 and later known as the Pentium processor. The P5 would have to provide 100 percent software compatibility and run all existing 486 software but should offer much higher performance at a much lower price. We were simply following Moore's Law! I was convinced that we could build a much better engine inside our next chip using the best possible microarchitecture techniques. That chip would achieve better performance than the RISC competition, and yet offer 100 percent software compatibility by staying with the same instruction set. These were major technical challenges that the team had to solve.

INVENT THE SUPERSCALAR TECHNOLOGY

Uri Weiser, a bright architect in our Haifa, Israel, development center, had been thinking about ways to accomplish these goals. He came up with a novel "superscalar" concept for the P5. Instead of executing one instruction per clock as RISC technology did, the new engine would execute two instructions per clock using two separate execution units. This would make our chip run almost twice as fast as RISC chips at the time. It was a very exciting idea. The trick was to employ this new superscalar engine to run the Intel architecture instruction set while minimizing complexity.

All the RISC advocates were convinced that the only way to dramatically improve performance was to switch to a new instruction set, which had the major disadvantage of breaking software compatibility. Uri felt that they were wrong. He worked with some of our key architects in Santa Clara to build a software simulator that showed how this new microarchitecture would work. Amazingly, the simulator demonstrated that this novel idea could in fact give us the performance levels we wanted running the Intel instruction set. It was a big technical breakthrough. The team convinced us that the instruction set was not necessarily tied to the underlying microarchitecture engine. This conceptual breakthrough allowed us to keep the same instruction set while redesigning the engine inside the chip to achieve better performance. Moreover, one could dramatically improve the performance of the same instruction set by inventing a new microarchitecture engine inside the chip.

BUILD THE DEVELOPMENT TEAM

We quickly formed a new team to focus solely on P5 development, separate from ongoing 486 efforts. We instituted a two-in-a-box management structure, with John Crawford focusing on the microarchitecture design and Avtar Saini directing chip implementation. Avtar had emigrated from India and was one of the key engineering managers on the 486 project. He was a strong driver with a very positive attitude. The two-in-a-box management structure was another Intel innovation. Very often a job is so complex that having two people share the same job offers a fitting solution to a tough problem. This type of management works when the two people have complementary skills and each has a clear area of responsibility. The two must have strong respect for each other and be in constant communication so that they are synchronized on key issues. I personally had several two-in-a-box management experiences, notably with Dave House and then Paul Otellini. In both cases, the team worked well. It also worked well in the case of John and Avtar. However, in some cases, the two-in-a-box structure failed, because the two individuals had too much overlap in skills and responsibilities, and they bumped into each other all the time. And sometimes the two people would compete with each other rather than cooperate as a team.

Avtar and John quickly recruited most of the 486 engineers onto the P5 project. Previously, many good experienced chip designers left Intel after completing a big project, because there was not another exciting project for them to work on. But the P5 was a very exciting project. John carefully placed each member of the 486 project team into P5 assignments that were right for them. This extra effort helped greatly in retaining key people and preserving our critical knowledge base.

There were reports that Sun was attempting this same superscalar approach for its next processor, called Super SPARC. So we were off in a race to see who would bring a superscalar chip to market first. Intel formed several marketing/engineering teams to talk to key customers and software companies and solicit their ideas on what features they would like to have in this new processor. Of course, they all wanted software compatibility and higher performance. They also told us that multiprocessing was really important—that one to four processors should work together to increase system performance, particularly in server computing. We responded to their requests and incorporated many key multiprocessing features into the P5 and the PCI chip set. Many other suggestions from our customers were also incorporated into the P5.

Because this processor required two execution units to implement the superscalar microarchitecture and included many new features to support our customers' requests, its complexity grew dramatically. The 486 utilized one million transistors; the P5 required more than three million transistors to implement all the architectural innovations. As a result, the chip development became extremely challenging and difficult. The size of the team grew to more than 100 people. In addition to recruiting and training lots of new people, keeping the whole team synchronized at all times was very challenging. We understood the critical importance of constant communications within the team. We instituted weekly meetings for the entire team, so that everyone understood the status of the project and the key focus areas for the following week. This process worked really well.

In developing the 486, we were able to incorporate many of the well-known architecture ideas from computer research, such as cache memory and floating-point processing. In the case of the P5, the superscalar and multiprocessing ideas were brand-new technologies, requiring the team to invent new techniques to implement these features. In addition, to achieve the necessary performance, we had to drive the chip's operating speed to very high levels, which stressed the circuit design to the limits. In order to design a three-million-transistor chip, we had to develop new CAD tools to do things that had never been done before. We were pushing limits in all areas to reach a technology peak that no one had scaled before. We had done that before in the development of the 486 and the 386. However, the task of designing this very complex P5 with an entirely new microarchitecture appeared really formidable. For some, this undertaking was too difficult, and they dropped out in the middle of the project. Others kept pushing forward relentlessly. I was convinced that it took a special kind of person who thrived on challenges to succeed with a project as big and complex as the P5. It was like going to the moon or climbing Mount Everest for the first time. The tasks were incredibly difficult and exhausting, yet the highs associated with accomplishing these unbelievable feats were tremendously motivating.

By the middle of 1991, the chip size was growing, which made me very uncomfortable. I asked the team to go through a "die diet" process by which all unnecessary features were cut so that the chip size would be contained within reasonable limits. We had to reduce the size of the internal level-one cache and remove many nice features. Even with all the dieting exercises, the chip ended up being quite a bit larger than the 486. Though the goal was to complete the chip by Christmas of 1991, allowing everyone to have a year-end vacation, the task was simply too big and complex. We eventually finished the chip in April 1992. Everyone was exhausted toward the end—most of them were working 12- to 16-hour days, often through weekends. We held a big pizza party to celebrate the completion of the chip design; everyone was so relieved to reach this major milestone. There was no doubt that we were making history by completing the world's first three-million-transistor chip. The news of the P5 design completion spread quickly through Silicon Valley. We even got congratulatory e-mail from Sun engineers. It was amazing how fast the information traveled.

Sun actually completed its Super SPARC chip design before us but had great difficulties making it work. We pulled ahead by quickly getting samples to customers who were able to start their PC system designs. Because of the complexity of its chip, Sun could not get the Super SPARC to work at higher than 40 MHz for at least six months. The P5 came out working at 60 MHz, and our team worked hard to get it to 66 MHz very quickly. We were pulling ahead of our competition!

All of a sudden, not only was the 486 DX2 processor faster than the first-generation SPARC, but our P5 outperformed the second-generation SPARC. Who said RISC was simple and fast? It was clear to many people by 1992 that the RISC promise was mostly hype. RISC processors actually grew in complexity and, in the end, were much more expensive and difficult to develop and sustain than their advocates promised. The reality was, we were able to use our innovative microarchitecture techniques, coupled with advanced silicon technologies, to outperform RISC chips such as SPARC, MIPS, and PowerPC. Given that, why would anybody want to switch from Intel architecture? No one did.

WHAT'S IN A NAME?

By mid-1992, we had the P5 chip working and were planning to bring it to the marketplace. We turned our attention to what we should call it: the 586? At that time, AMD was beginning to sample its imitation 486 product, the AM486. It became clear to us that the 386, 486, and other X86 product names were so popular that imitators were taking advantage of the name to market their products. We had spent huge amounts of marketing and advertising money to build equity in product names that others used for free. What should we do? There were only two choices: go with the 586 as a logical sequence, or call it something totally different. Changing the established naming sequence would require huge public relations and advertising efforts to establish the new brand name. There was also the big risk that the new name might not catch on, which would be a major problem for us.

Andy finally decided that we must name the P5 something else and proactively obsolete the X86 name to gain trademark protection over a new name. We formed a team to come up with the right name. We even started a naming contest for all Intel employees and encouraged everyone to submit ideas. We had never before named a product by a word rather than by a number. We were taking a huge risk in abandoning a well-established naming convention and moving to an unknown brand name. But we all agreed that it was the right thing to do, and we charged ahead.

What's in a name? Actually, it is one of the most important aspects of a product. Simple, memorable names stick in consumers' minds. In the crowded marketplace where you are required to distinguish your product against so many others, a great name is essential. The P5 naming team conducted extensive market research to test various alternatives. We decided to unveil the name in early November 1992, just before the big Comdex trade show in Las Vegas. A week before the announcement, Andy called a meeting of about 20 people, who were all sworn to secrecy. The naming team explained the process they followed in coming up with different choices, showed us the pros and cons of the leading candidates, and then presented three finalists. We had an extensive discussion, with everyone expressing their preferences. Andy took a lot of notes. I actually liked all three names but picked one and stated why I liked it. After everyone spoke, Andy thanked us and left the room. The decision was clearly his, and he labored over it that weekend, talking to Dennis Carter many times. In fact, they flip-flopped a few times on their choice. Andy finally made a decision just before he departed for New York. The following week, Andy appeared on a network TV news interview in New York City and told the world that our next microprocessor would be called the Pentium processor. The reaction was swift: most people liked it. It was a new word. It sounded like an element, like helium or aluminum. We monitored how well the new name was accepted by counting the number of times the Pentium name was mentioned versus 586. Within three months, there were more mentions of the Pentium processor than the 586. The name was enjoying great acceptance, and we were all relieved. We were on track to obsolete not only our own products but their names! A gutsy move indeed.

By early 1993, many pieces were falling into place for the Pentium processor. The name was accepted and the chip was moving into production. Our PCI chip set came out at the same time as the processor, and it provided really great graphics and system-level performance for Pentium processor–based PCs. Our next step was to introduce the Pentium processor to the world. We did that in two big steps. We first unveiled the Pentium processor technology at the CEBIT show in Hanover, Germany, in March 1993. Then we announced the pricing and availability in May in the United States. At the technology launch at CEBIT, we featured many Pentium processor–based systems demonstrating new and exciting applications for business and home, including the futuristic virtual reality software. Enthusiasm for the product and the technology was extremely high. The weather in Hanover was cold, but the excitement over the Pentium processor was red hot! We were elated with the great reception the world was giving our new baby—the Pentium processor.

RACE AHEAD OF THE COMPETITION

We had many strong competitors for our Pentium processor. By the end of 1992, though SPARC and MIPS had faded in the marketplace, the PowerPC camp began to mount a major marketing campaign against the Pentium processor. The first PowerPC chip, the 601, was just completed and being touted as faster, cheaper, and cooler than the Pentium processor. Big ads everywhere pushed the PowerPC as the new and exciting chip that would overtake the Pentium processor. Borrowing a page from Intel's successful Crush campaign of 1980, IBM showed the PowerPC road map over the next few years, with the 603, 604, and 620 processors offering increasing levels of performance. Apple began to use the PowerPC to replace the Motorola 68000 for its new PowerMac line, introduced in early 1994. John Scully, then president of Apple, was making boastful public predictions that Apple would ship ten times more PowerPC-based machines than Intel would ship Pentium processors within the first year. The reality was just the other way around: by the end of 1994, Pentium processors outshipped PowerPCs by ten to one.

We were determined to push the Pentium processor's performance far beyond that of the PowerPC. As we did with the 486 processors, we had the Portland design team move the Pentium processor to the next-generation 0.6-micron technology (the first-generation Pentium processor that operated at 66 MHz was on 0.8-micron technology) to create faster and lower-power products. We began this project in early 1992. The market for mobile computers was growing fast, and it was important that we offer Pentium processors with battery operation capabilities for the mobile market. Therefore, the team added special power-saving features so the product could be used for notebook computers. The project went very well, and we had the first products out by the end of 1993. We decided to repeat the strategy we had used with the 486: show off the very highest performance achievable for the Pentium processor, to outrun the challenger, the PowerPC. In February 1994, Joe Schutz presented a technical paper at the International Solid State Circuit Conference on the achievement of a 150-MHz Pentium processor, showing once again that the Pentium processor outperformed the RISC chips and had performance headroom to spare. He astonished the audience with an onstage demonstration of a 150-MHz Pentium processor–based system running real applications. The PowerPC people were shocked and dismayed, just as the SPARC people had been in 1991 when Joe presented the 100-MHz 486 paper. We shattered their claims that the PowerPC would be faster and cheaper. On the contrary, the Pentium processor was far ahead of the PowerPC in performance.

It is one thing to demonstrate a high-performance Pentium processor, but our real job was to deliver high-volume, high-performance Pentium processors in production. We surprised our competition by introducing the 100-MHz Pentium processors in March 1994 for volume production, just one month before Apple introduced the desktop Power Mac at 60 and 80 MHz. We stole the desktop performance thunder from them, in spite of all the performance claims they had been making. All of a sudden, the Power-PC camp was on the defensive. On the mobile computer side, Toshiba was the first to announce in October 1994 a Pentium processor–based mobile computer, which became an instant success. We had many companies building notebook PCs with 75-MHz Pentium processors, taking advantage of the power-saving features we had incorporated into the Pentium processor. Although the PowerPC camp promised a 603 chip designed especially for notebook computers, they could not deliver on the promise. Because we were able to lead in both high performance and low power, the Pentium processor became by far the volume leader for both desktop and mobile PCs.

We continued to push the performance higher and higher to satisfy the insatiable demands of end-user. By the end of 1996, we were able to double the speed, shipping large volumes of 200-MHz Pentium processors, far ahead of what the competition was doing. In spite of their earlier bold claims, the PowerPC delivered little and had only two customers: Apple and IBM. Their volumes remained modest. On February 10, 1997, Microsoft announced that it had decided to pull the plug on Windows NT development for the PowerPC, perhaps ending

IBM's and Apple's dream of making the PowerPC a broadly used chip family for computing.

HOME COMPUTING BECOMES A REALITY

Several exciting developments happened at about the same time in late 1993. Along with Pentium processors and PCI chip sets, CD-ROMs with big storage capacities and sound cards with high-quality sound became available. Many PCs incorporated these new technologies, turning them into full multimedia PCs and bringing a whole new set of capabilities to end-user. This ignited an explosion in exciting CD-ROM-based multimedia applications. Running these new multimedia applications with acceptable speed and interactivity required a Pentium processor–based PC. Multimedia PCs at last brought truly useful and exciting applications to the home.

For example, one of the hottest-selling applications in 1993 was a CD-ROM-based encyclopedia. Not only was it much easier to search for the information that one wanted, but it was exciting to be able to see video clips and hear sounds associated with the subject matter. The information was much richer, and updating was easy: you simply replaced the old CD with a new one or downloaded the latest information from the Internet. And it was small—a tiny lightweight disc rather than a dozen heavy volumes. And this was just one of many exciting new applications made possible by the multimedia PC. In addition, many people wanted a PC at home that was compatible with the one in the office so that they could bring work home. They were using PCs for writing checks, doing the family's taxes, playing games, sending and receiving electronic mail, and accessing the Internet. With all these useful applications, the home PC market finally took off. By the end of 1993, a full 30 percent of PCs sold in the United States were destined for the home.

Multimedia software ran much better on Pentium processor–based PCs because of the superior graphics capabilities that came with the

PCI chip set. All these developments were happening at once. Home and business PC users were demanding Pentium-based PCs, rather than the older 486-based PCs. The new Pentium processor had rendered our own 486 processors obsolete. That was fine by us. We dramatically increased Pentium processor production to satisfy the huge demand. Andy Grove emphasized to the whole company that our "job one" was to ramp the Pentium processor as quickly as possible. The winners were end-users, who got higher-performance PCs at lower prices. The Pentium processor ramp was ultimately four times faster than our 486 ramp.

START THE NEXT TWO GENERATIONS

We began developing the Pentium processor after the 486 chip was completed. There were several problems with this serial development. First, it was difficult to remove people from the previous project, as they were busy getting that product into production. As a result, the start of the Pentium processor development was delayed by at least six months. Second, as most of our design talent came from the 486 team, it was natural for them to extend ideas they used on the 486 rather than taking more radical approaches. In fact, it took Uri Weiser from Israel to inject the superscalar idea into the Santa Clara team. Third, because of the "die diets" we went through with the P5 project, a lot of good ideas ended up on the "cutting room floor." Many of these ideas would be lost if they were not used in another product.

In addition to these internal factors, we saw more and more competitive pressures from RISC challengers and imitators of Intel-architecture processors. All these reasons compelled us to accelerate our development process even further to push past our competitors and to obsolete our own products faster. Several people suggested doing parallel development, that is, starting the next-generation chip before the Pentium processor was completed. The idea sounded very appealing. The key was the availability of an experienced chip design team that could take on the big task. We happened to have just that in 1991. Our design team in Portland, Oregon, had just developed the 486 DX2. It was natural to ask that team to take on the next design, code-named P6, in parallel to the P5 development. And we did.

INVENT THE DYNAMIC EXECUTION TECHNOLOGY

Fred Pollack, an experienced senior architect who had worked on the BIIN project, joined the P6 team in 1991 to start building the architecture department for the P6. Fred is a brilliant architect with a very creative mind. Fred built a very good team of architects with recruits from inside and outside of Intel. One of the talents that Fred recruited, Bob Colwell, became the chief architect of the P6 in mid-1992, when Fred moved on to the job of planning the whole microprocessor product line. Bob is a very bright architect and strong leader with a great sense of humor. Bob and his team worked intensely to come up with a new microarchitecture that would surpass the performance of RISC processors, yet provide complete compatibility with our existing software base. They learned from the Pentium team's experiences and came up with several innovative ideas. Many of their early meetings were held in a big closet so no one could distract them. By early 1992, the P6 architecture was taking shape and looking very exciting.

Among the team's revolutionary ideas was a technology called "Dynamic Execution" (DE), whereby each instruction does not have to wait for the completion of the previous one, as in conventional processor design, but can jump ahead. Dynamic Execution can be compared to people shopping in a supermarket. If each shopper had to follow the shopper ahead of her in a prescribed route through the supermarket aisles, the line would bog down, with some people wanting to take more time at one station, causing everyone else to wait. In a supermaket, you can simply roll your cart past the dawdler. Why not let the processor's instructions do the same?—i.e., jump ahead. Older processors were designed to operate "in order." The Dynamic Execution scheme allowed some instructions to skip ahead of a previous instruction, which might be stuck waiting for data, for example. This naturally improved the overall operating speed. In fact, this new scheme was way ahead of any RISC ideas at the time. When I first heard about the concept, I was convinced it was the right approach. This new technique would pull us far ahead of our competition. I was concerned, though, about how to implement this brand-new architecture without adding unnecessary complexity.

It was not enough just to speed up the microprocessor. PC performance was often limited by the processor-to-memory communication speed. The P6 team came up with another new creation: the "Dual Independent Bus" (DIB). Instead of only one bus between the processor and memory as in the Pentium processor and the 486, why not have two buses: a "frontside" bus to the main memory and a "backside" bus to the cache memory. This innovation dramatically improves the processor-to-memory speed, and the result is much improved server and workstation performance which is often more limited in a one-bus system. DIB also allows multiprocessor systems to scale up to more than four processors in a system for high-performance servers. In order to implement the DIB, we had to design a new cache memory chip and a new chip set, in addition to designing the microprocessor. In essence, we had to design a whole new computing platform, not just a new processor. This was totally consistent with our microprocessor strategy all along: we must offer the total product and not just one device.

The combination of DE and DIB not only provides enhanced performance for the classic desktop and mobile PC needs but also makes the P6 an ideal processor for the new and fast-growing workstation and server markets. We were very happy with what the team came up with: a P6 chip and system that would grow our business into many segments. The P6 product would be a giant step ahead of our first Pentium processor, which we were already planning to obsolete.

During the P6 architecture creation, regular reviews on its progress and the start of the design process were held in Portland. In parallel to the architecture work going on, we recruited a very experienced chip design manager, Randy Steck, to head up the P6 chip design effort. Randy is one of the most organized and process-oriented managers we've ever had. Starting with a small core team, Randy recruited and built up a world-class design organization of several hundred people in about 18 months. This project was much more complex than the Pentium processor project, and the transistor count came in at close to six million, twice that of the Pentium processor. No one had ever attempted to build a chip of this complexity before. We were off to climb the next mountain peak.

MAKE THE P6 A REALITY

Around the middle of 1992, we had a good idea of what the P6 would look like, and we were riding high. With all these innovative ideas, we would deliver unbelievable performance to PC users and be way ahead of our competition! Very quickly, however, the euphoria of our architectural dreams met the cold, hard reality of implementation, and we came down to earth fast. Pat Gelsinger, who had been leading the P6 team, was asked to head up Intel's new video conferencing business (subsequently known as Intel ProShare® technology). I was sorry to see him go, but it presented a good growth opportunity for him. I decided to move a strong engineering manager from Israel, Dadi Perlmutter, to be the P6 general manager. Dadi had designed some of our most successful math co-processors, including the 387, and he was bright and showed tremendous attention to details. It was risk-taking on my part, as Dadi had never managed a team of several hundred people, and he would have to learn quickly how to operate in Portland, which was quite different from Israel. But I had a lot of confidence in him and promised to work closely with him and support him with lots of coaching. Dadi moved his family to Portland in November 1992 and hit the ground running. He faced quite a few challenges. The chip complexity was much greater than anyone had predicted. The chip size was getting very big, and the power consumption was too high. The team went through four very painful "die diets" to cut features, simplify architecture, and reduce power consumption. As a result, the schedule was pushed out about six months, and I was not happy about that at all.

By June of 1993, the logic design was finally complete, which was a major milestone. The team was exhausted, and there was much anxiety about when the chip would be completed. We decided to hold an ice cream celebration. On the plane to Portland, I thought about what to say to the team. The biggest challenge still lay ahead: to take all that logic and cram it into silicon in one year—a huge task. If we failed, our competition would have a field day. If we succeeded, we would stun the world with a product so revolutionary that it would be an unbelievable success.

It occurred to me that I should paint pictures of success so the team could visualize what it would feel like; I hoped this would be a big motivator for them. On June 25, 1993, the whole team gathered in the cafeteria to celebrate the completion of the logic design. Everybody was eating ice cream and having a good time. I got up and congratulated them on the wonderful job they had done on the logic design. Then I said, "I want to show you what you should expect to see in the future." My first slide said, "Intel Unveils the World's Fastest Chip: the P6 at ISSCC [International Solid State Circuit Conference] in February 1995." People applauded. My next slide showed a hypothetical *Wall Street Journal* headline: "Intel Introduces Revolutionary P6 That Blows Away RISC," dated May 1995. Everyone cheered. Then I showed the last slide: "Hawaiian Islands invaded by vacationing P6 celebrities who just completed the world's most incredible microprocessor," dated June 1995. The whole place went wild. They all wanted to see the headlines become reality, and they all wanted to take that exotic vacation!

Many members of the team came to me and asked what it would take to get them such great vacations. I told them I would make a bet with them: if the team delivered the P6 product with specified performance, cost, and time schedules, they would win the bet and the vacation. The team quickly came up with a matrix showing these criteria and establishing a point system. For 12 points or higher (great accomplishments), they would win an exotic vacation; for 9–11 points (good results), they would have a weekend celebration at a place within driving distance; for 5–8 points (mediocre results), they would have a pizza party; for 0–4 points (poor results), they would have bed and breakfast in the Folsom Prison (this is a well-known California prison, but Intel also has a facility in the city of Folsom). We actually held a town hall–type meeting with the whole team to officially agree to the bet. They were all confident they would win. What a dramatic emotional turnaround for a team that could clearly visualize success!

It was not all smooth sailing after the bet was made, but the team really pulled together to make this incredibly challenging chip happen. We had lots of tense moments toward the summer of 1994 when the chip design was supposed to be completed. Many issues pushed the schedule out month by month. One of the team's major milestones was to show me a demo of a P6 system by the end of 1994. When the September milestone was missed, there was lots of high anxiety. By November, when the Pentium floating-point issue (discussed in Chapter 6) surfaced, the P6 design was finally completed. At this time, I was totally immersed in the Pentium processor floating-point crisis.

By December 21, the Pentium floating-point crisis had abated. The P6 team told me they had just received the first P6 silicon, and it was

FIGURE 13   **MICROPROCESSOR REPORT**

MICROPROCESSOR ◇ REPORT
THE INSIDERS' GUIDE TO MICROPROCESSOR HARDWARE

VOLUME 9   NUMBER 15   NOVEMBER 13, 1995

Intel Boosts Pentium Pro to 200 MHz
Integer Performance Beats the Best RISCs

by Michael Slater

After nearly a year of buildup, Intel has formally announced its Pentium Pro processor and demonstrated performance that makes it the clear leader for integer applications. For the first time in the history of the x86 architecture, Intel is in a performance leadership position, creating a renewed challenge for its struggling RISC competitors.

Source: Microprocessor Report

working great. They wanted to give me a demonstration on Friday, December 23, 1994. I was pleasantly surprised by the news and flew up to Portland, still exhausted from the month-long crisis. More than 20 people were crammed into the small lab, and all I saw were smiling faces. The screen of the P6-powered computer was flashing one message: "The P6 is working. We won the bet, Albert!" They excitedly pointed out the P6 chip in the system and ran through several applications to show that it was really working. Even at this early stage, it was already running faster than the Pentium processor. I thought I was the happiest person on earth at that moment. They were able to get first silicon out and put together a demonstration system in just one week, an unbelievable accomplishment. What a team!! At that moment, I realized that, although the Pentium processor was just ramping in volume, its successor had just been born: the P6. By starting parallel development, we accomplished precisely what we set out to do—accelerate the development of our new products.

From that moment on, the P6 story unfolded almost exactly as I had "imagined" it with the team on June 25, 1993. Bob Colwell presented a great paper on the P6 architecture at the February 1995 ISSCC conference, and the RISC guys were stunned by what we had accomplished. We had surpassed them once again! The *Microprocessor Report* carried a front-page story titled, "P6 Underscores Intel's Lead," in its February 16, 1995, issue, right after the conference. We named the first member of the P6 family the Pentium Pro processor, preserving the equity in the Pentium name. We introduced the product in November 1995, and the press, including the *Wall Street Journal, PC Week,* and other leading business and industry publications, gave it rave reviews. By the second half of 1996, the demand for the Pentium Pro processor was so high that the gray-market price was $200 higher than the list price. It was another home run for us. We also quickly moved on to develop the second member of the P6 family, the Pentium II, and ramp that product aggressively in volume.

So what happened to the bet? By February 1995, we agreed to hold a big meeting to officially score the bet. We set it up like a trial in an English court. I was dressed as the judge with white wig and

FIGURE 14   THE PENTIUM PRO PROCESSOR

Source: Intel

black robe. For each milestone, a witness was called to present the case for the appropriate points earned. In some cases, counterpoints were argued. When the total points were added up, the score was 11, one point shy of the winning score. The team moaned. Then Dadi Perlmutter, the division general manager, argued convincingly that the P6 performance far exceeded the original expectations, and for this I should give them an extra point. I thought about it for more than a minute. Several hundred people held their breath; I could hear a pin drop. Finally, I rose to address the team. I congratulated them for a phenomenal accomplishment. I told them that, in addition to the higher performance that Dadi raised, they had exceeded everyone's expectations in terms of design quality, as evidenced by the low production defect levels. As a result, I would award them the extra point—they had won the bet. The whole place erupted with cheers! Not only had they won the bet, but they had created the microprocessor of the decade.

One of the inevitable consequences of Moore's Law is that if you don't drive to obsolete your own products, someone else will do it for you and leave you behind. The next new product must meet clear business objectives both for us and for customers. For Intel, the most important objective is software compatibility, which offers software investment protection for our customers. In the face of strong competition that tried to pull people to adopt new software bases, we have stuck to our conviction of providing software compatibility while employing our technical capabilities to offer better and better products. Our customers are the winners. We have consistently obsoleted our own products, and we intend to obsolete the first Pentium processor with the P6 family of products: the Pentium Pro processor and the Pentium II processor. And, of course, we are working hard on the next generation to obsolete these in a few years.

CHAPTER ELEVEN

LEARN AND BE
THE BEST

INNOVATION AND CONSTANT CHANGE ARE THE ESSENCES OF THE HIGH-
technology business. Furthermore, Moore's Law says that the rate of
innovation and change actually accelerates over time. The Internet
is a good example. Since it burst on the scene in 1995, new products
and new ways of doing business on the Internet spring up every day.
This rapid rate of change demands that people and companies must
stay on a path of constant learning—about the environment, about
new technologies, and about new business practices. We continue
to learn and to relentlessly push the frontier of digital technology.
We also continue to learn and to push the frontier of management
technology.

CONSTANT LEARNING

LEARN TO LEARN

Professor William Spicer's research group at Stanford University offered
a rich experience of learning for many graduate students, I among them.
Bill Spicer, now the Stanford Ashcerman Professor of Engineering,
Emeritus, joined the Stanford faculty from RCA Labs in 1961 and set
up a unique photo emissions laboratory. He organized the lab like a
small company and took on the role of CEO: providing direction for his

group, securing funding, and dealing with external audiences. His four senior graduate students coached and supervised the junior graduate students.

When Bill suggested that I write my Ph.D. thesis on the optical properties of ferromagnetic metals like cobalt and its nonferromagnetic neighbors like palladium and platinum, I replied that I knew nothing about the topic. He looked me in the eye and said, "I don't either, but I bet you can do some research and become an expert in no time." I did what he suggested: talked to fellow students and other faculty members and researched the relevant literature. Bill was right. Within a few months, I learned a lot about the optical properties of these metals and felt comfortable about this brand new area. That was a good experience. It taught me that it is perfectly OK not to know something. Go find out and become an expert. Why not?

About nine months after I began my research, Bill pulled me into his office and said, "I want you to present your research results at the next American Physical Society meeting in Los Angeles in two months." I was in shock, and said, "Wow, my experimental results are not all there, and I have never spoken at a conference. I even get nervous speaking in the classroom!" Bill laughed and said, "Well, you have two months to pull together your data, and that's lots of time. By the way, it will be good for you to gain experience in public speaking. The key is to be really well prepared and to think through all the tough questions that may come up."

Bill was doing what a good manager does: setting high goals that made me stretch and giving me specific coaching on how to achieve those goals. After lots of hard work and burning the midnight oil, my data were completed and summarized. Then I practiced my speech dozens of times privately and also in front of fellow graduate students and Bill. They helped a great deal by coming up with tough questions the audience might ask. By the time I went on stage to speak, I was thoroughly prepared and felt confident. After the talk, there was only one easy question, one I had anticipated. That experience gave me a big boost of confidence in public speaking. Bill Spicer was right in pushing his students to practice public speaking early. He encouraged us to practice and improve our skills by presenting papers at many occasions such as regional American Physical Society conferences and Stanford seminars. The ability to present effectively in meetings and at conferences is a valuable skill for anyone in a high-technology industry.

Bill Spicer also coached his students on how to write clear and logical technical papers and theses. He would review our drafts and send them back with red pen marks everywhere, asking us to explain more clearly and simply, to reorganize our contents, and to present a crisp abstract and a conclusion. We typically labored over three or four drafts before the paper was done. The technical content of our thesis work and papers was not necessarily relevant to our work later. But Bill Spicer's coaching on learning, teamwork, public speaking, and writing benefited us significantly for years.

LEARN TO MANAGE

Three years after I started my first job at Fairchild R&D, my boss, Ed Snow, asked me to be a section manager in the physics department, overseeing five other research engineers. I asked Ed, "How do I become a manager?" He told me that I should take some courses at nearby business schools and the American Management Association. My job was to make sure the research programs of these five people proceeded well. These researchers were doing independent work, so my task was very simple. I spent some time talking with them about their work and offering suggestions, but I pretty much left them alone. I followed Ed's advice and read some books on management, took several management classes, and found that the material made a lot of sense to me. I spent very little time actually managing the researchers and instead spent more than 50 percent of my time on my own research. I was a rank beginner in management.

At my first job at Intel, the situation was totally different. My team was small—only three people—but we had an important task: to convert the whole production line from two-inch to three-inch wafers so that we could double the output. Although the team had a common goal, we were each working on different parts of the problem. But our work had to fit together, and we had to carefully document our work for manufacturing and train the operators to do their new jobs. We collaborated closely with the design engineers to make sure all 1103 memory characteristics would remain the same on the new process. We had to work closely with reliability engineers to make sure the new production process produced reliable results. In essence, we had to interact with many groups within the company to make sure the program was successful. This had not been the case at Fairchild, where all the researchers were doing independent work that needed little coordination with one another or with other groups. No wonder the management job at Fairchild was easy! We learned on the job at Intel about what we had to do: how to set goals, how to get all members of a team marching in the same direction, and how to interact with all parts of a company to make the program successful.

In the early days of Intel, many of us were still novices in management. Andy Grove has been the driving force in developing our own management system. We held our first development session in 1973, with the whole senior management team of about twenty attending. That four-day session really set the tone for inventing the management system at Intel. We invited some outside speakers to give us a framework for our discussions. Then we took charge of the session ourselves. We identified the management problems that we needed to solve. We attacked these problems by forming small groups of six to seven people to brainstorm, discuss, and debate solutions to specific problems, and come up with a set of concrete recommendations. Then, each group presented its findings in a summary session, followed by thorough discussions. Finally, we pulled together all the proposals and agreed on a chosen path. From these intensely interactive sessions, we came up with unique and novel ways of managing our business.

One of the most important outcomes of this first management session was the Intel Management by Objective (iMBO) system, which later became Management by Planning (MBP). The iMBO process was invaluable in carrying out our results orientation, discipline, and risk-taking culture. Following our first session in 1973, the top twenty or so senior managers would go off-site once a year for three to four days to refresh our management practices and system. Every time we met, we came up with many new ideas that we would incorporate into our management system.

One of the most memorable management development sessions for me was Paul Hersey's talk about situational leadership, a concept he had developed in a book on the same subject.[21] He categorized workplace situations and appropriate leadership styles into four quadrants:

1. High task, low relationship
2. High task, high relationship
3. Low task, high relationship
4. Low task, low relationship

He showed us the film *Twelve O'Clock High* with Gregory Peck, about a new military commander taking over a demoralized team during the war. It showed the change in the commander's leadership style as the team's situation evolved. At the outset, he applied the first-quadrant style, acting like a dictator and forcing discipline into the team in order to push them out of self-pity and into action. As the men gained more confidence and started generating their own ideas, he switched to quadrant-two and quadrant-three styles that were more participatory and less dictatorial. Toward the end of the movie, the commander became even more laid back, in quadrant-four style, as the team was really going on its own and needed only occasional guidance.

This session was instrumental in teaching us that, although everyone has a predominant leadership style, we have to be able to "switch modes" if we want to be effective in different situations. We were so impressed with this session that we developed a course at Intel on situational leadership, which most of our managers have taken over the years.

Constant learning is a must for everybody at Intel and at other high-technology businesses. To handle the need for ongoing training for all employees, not just managers, we set up Intel University around 1975. Here, both technical and management classes are taught, mostly by Intel managers. I have always felt that the best way to learn is to teach. I have participated in most of the management development sessions at Intel and taught many classes. The classes that constitute the cornerstones of Intel's management system are "Management by Planning" (MBP), "Constructive Confrontation," "Performance Appraisal," "Effective Meetings," "Participatory Decision Making," and "Situational Management."

"Management by Planning" is the key to our results-oriented culture. This class teaches employees how to set objectives and key results that can be measured concretely. For example, a goal of completing product design and shipping one million units by March 31st is specific and measurable. A poor goal might be, "Hold three meetings to discuss the marketing plan." This is a description of activity but not results. One could hold an infinite number of meetings to talk about the marketing plan but never produce one. MBP has been an excellent process for getting the various parts of the company to align their action plans so that everyone works toward the same overall goals.

"Constructive Confrontation" teaches how to confront issues in a positive manner without getting into personal attacks. Being open, confronting problems head on, and solving them quickly are key elements of Intel's culture. The goal is to focus on the data and facts and less on opinion.

We teach a course on giving performance appraisals, because it is important to teach managers not only how to assess the performance of their subordinates, but how to coach them proactively with constructive suggestions for improvement. A manager should give specific examples of poor performance and be clear about what constitutes good performance. Telling a subordinate, "Your presentation was bad. You're not good at this sort of thing," immediately puts the individual on the defensive and does nothing to help him improve. A good manager might say, "Your speech left several people confused about your message. John said he didn't understand exactly what you wanted him to do. Kim asked me what you meant. Note what Mike did. He used one simple slide to put his messages across clearly and crisply. You need to do the same or better!" The person gets the message that his presentation was poor, but he also gets specific feedback on what he needs to do to improve.

In the "Effective Meetings" course, we teach the specifics of holding meetings that result in concrete results and actions. We stress the importance of publishing an agenda and a purpose for your meeting ahead of time and of having the right people at your meeting. Allowing ten minutes or so at the end of a meeting to summarize the conclusions and next steps gives everyone a clear sense of the meeting's outcome.

In "Participatory Decision-Making," we identify the key steps in any decision: define the decision clearly; decide when the decision must be made; identify the decision-maker and the ratifier; define the leader of the decision-making team; and define the participants. A decision meeting is held and the final decision clearly communicated to all parties involved.

In "Situational Management," we teach how to apply appropriate management styles to different situations. The first step is to analyze the situation. For example, when I was first promoted to section manager at Fairchild, the research engineers were all mature, competent individuals. As a result, my quadrant-four style was just about right. I must admit, I practiced this style out of ignorance rather than intent. If I had known better, the more appropriate style would have been quadrant three. I should have forged a stronger relationship with my people and thus encouraged more cooperation between them to produce more coherent research.

These are our foundation courses. Through the years, we've significantly expanded our curriculum. The Intel University puts together week-long seminars for first-line, middle, and senior managers. These sessions offer lectures and working sessions, and they also provide an excellent environment for people from different parts of the company to get to know each other, which can be invaluable later on. In addition to management classes, each of the major organizations puts together more specialized technical courses like how use CAD tools and how to do high-performance circuit design. In the microprocessor organization, where we hire many new people every year directly out of school, we put together special classes for these new college graduates so that they can learn and adapt to how we do things rapidly and efficiently. Training is one of the most important things we do, because it is a key avenue to continuous learning.

LEARN TO BE A GENERAL MANAGER

In 1990, we recruited and promoted a great group of seven to eight divisional general managers in the Microprocessor Products Group. All of them were new to the job of general manager. The youngest was Pat Gelsinger, who was in charge of the P6 product line. The most seasoned was Hans Geyer, who was our sales manager in Europe. He had just moved into the factory as the general manager of the 486 microprocessors, with the express purpose of broadening his experience. The rest were somewhere in between. Each was responsible for a multimillion-dollar business at the heart of Intel.

My staff and I immediately saw the need to effectively train these people in the skills necessary to be good general managers. They were already undergoing intensive on-the-job training like everyone at Intel. I discussed the idea of a general manager (GM) training session, and the group loved it. We decided to conduct the training in a seminar format, with one six-hour session each month. Some sessions would include dinner to facilitate free discussions. Because general managers need to have a wide range of skills, the series was designed to cover a broad range of topics. I took on the job of organizing the training sessions, selecting the topics, recruiting the speakers and leading the group discussions. We started in September 1991 with the following outline:

What Does a GM Do?—David Yoffie
Finance for the New GM—Harold Hughes
Setting the Strategy: Case Studies of Crown Cork and Seal and Wal-Mart—David Yoffie
Directing Operations—Craig Barrett
Learning Organization—Peter Senge
Principle-Centered Leadership—Covey Leadership Center
External Communications—Andy Grove
Graduation

What does a general manager do? In simplest terms, he or she manages diverse functions such as engineering, marketing, and manufacturing, and drives these groups to work together to accomplish a common business goal. He or she is very much like a company president, except that he or she need not be concerned with corporate matters such as treasury or corporate legal issues.

David Yoffie, a professor at the Harvard Business School and a well-known authority on strategy, led the introductory session. David also serves on Intel's Board of Directors. In the first seminar, we examined the GM's role by examining a well-known CEO at the time. The most telling indicator of how well this person was doing his job was his calendar for two weeks. He spent lots of time on outside directorships, such as the United Way and business round tables. He attended several plant openings and celebrations and gave several awards. However, he spent no time on strategic formulation or operational matters. He did not see a single customer! We were shocked. He was publicly talking about transforming his company from old to new, but his calendar showed that he was operating like a ceremonial head and devoting no time to changing the course of his company. His actions did not match his words.

This case study showed what a GM should *not* do: be just a front guy. It also showed how important it is for a GM to set a clear strategy for an organization and a concrete course of actions for getting there. Soon after our session, this CEO was replaced. All the GMs in our class learned from this example, and none took on a large burden of outside ceremonial activities.

Finance for the new GM is fairly basic: profit and loss, inventory valuation, cost, and budgeting. However, basics are always important. I review our Plan of Record, including key accomplishments, problems, and finances, once a quarter with my GMs. I expect them to perform equal to or better than the plan. We also meet quarterly with the Executive Office—Andy Grove, Craig Barrett, and Gordon Moore—to go over the group's performance and financial matters.

The "Setting Strategy" session consisted of detailed case studies of two very successful companies: Crown Cork and Seal, and Wal-Mart. These companies were in industries far removed from ours, yet we learned many powerful lessons from them. We talked in detail about the definition of competitive strategy. The definition we took away was, "the goals and actions needed to achieve a sustainable advantage in a specific marketplace." The key words are "actions" and "sustainable." Often, companies publish lofty goals like "technology leadership" and "marketing leadership" without backing these goals up with concrete actions for making them happen.

Both Crown and Wal-Mart based their competitive strategies on cost; that is, they took concrete actions to achieve the lowest cost in their respective businesses. Wal-Mart became the largest retailer in the nation, with a chain of discount stores that overtook

Sears and K-mart by offering everyday low prices, friendly service, and leading-edge inventory controls. The real secret to making their low-cost strategy work was their state-of-the-art information system, which told them exactly where every piece of merchandise was and when it was sold. This enabled their distribution system to move merchandise with lightning speed to the right stores at the right time. Also, Wal-Mart's warehouse and transportation systems were the most efficient in the industry. Crown's key competitive strategy was to continuously reduce its administrative costs so they would have the highest margins in their industry.

In addition to the cost-based strategy, the other commonly used strategy is to differentiate products or service—to make them distinctive and unique. A good example is Mercedes-Benz, which offers clearly differentiated automobiles with distinctive engineering quality. Intel's strategy has been mostly to make differentiated products based on technological excellence. We keep our products a step or two ahead of the competition by devoting extensive resources to R&D and fostering an innovative environment. After studying these two case studies, however, we became much more cost-conscious and decided to achieve more competitive costs without deviating from our differentiation strategy. We put together a set of action plans to go after waste; since then, our microprocessor costs have dropped significantly.

"Directing Operations" was a session led by Craig Barrett, our chief operating officer at the time. Two key points jumped out. The first was that we really needed to understand a problem before jumping to a solution. Because of our results- and action-oriented culture, we all want to solve problems quickly. However, if we act before we understand a problem clearly we can end up with the wrong solution to the problem. Craig explained that we must understand the root cause of each problem before jumping in with solutions. As an example, Intel experienced a business slowdown in 1991, which caused us to worry about whether or not our marketing messages were clear enough for the volumes we wanted to ship. We talked with some of our key customers and end users about this issue. It turned out that business had slowed due to uncertainties over interest rates, and our marketing messages had nothing to do with it. Had we acted on impulse and altered our marketing messages, we would have confused the market rather than increasing our sales volume. It was a good reminder to think before you act.

The other key point we learned was that GMs needed to be in touch with reality at all times. We must see customers, talk to people at various levels in our organizations, and have a firsthand sense of what is going on. Information filtered through an organization tends to get watered down and lose its original meaning. One of the things Craig did to stay in touch with his organization was to go into the factory occasionally and work as an operator for a few hours. This really gave him a firsthand feel for conditions in his factory. All our GMs wanted to do something equally hands-on. Several went into the field and acted as salesmen for a few days, which gave them a clearer picture of the marketplace and customer needs. I increased the number of informal open lunches I have with fifteen to twenty invited people in all parts of my organization. These are great sessions that allow me to listen directly to what our employees have to say. People ask questions and talk openly about issues and concerns and are generally thrilled at the opportunity to get a sympathetic hearing from me. I've come away with a better sense of what's going on in my organization and often get ideas for how we can do better. I have also worked as a design engineer, architect, and CAD tools developer for two to four hours at a time as a team member. These sessions help me get a really good firsthand sense of the current conditions and possible areas for improvement.

The "Learning Organization" session was led by Peter Senge of MIT, who had just written an excellent book called *Fifth Discipline*,[22] which subsequently became a bestseller. His thesis was that we needed to understand the "whole system" and not just pieces of it. For example, when there is a delay in a system, the system is often slow to respond at first, and then it usually overshoots. This type of oscillation causes big problems for people who do not have a full understanding of the whole system. Since publishing *The Fifth Discipline* Senge has become very well known in management circles for his ideas about system-level understanding. We were fortunate to have him for a whole day to talk through his ideas. He also showed us that simple system behavior could be simulated by a computer.

It was an intriguing idea that one could model a real-life system by computer simulations to find out what would happen under different scenarios. In the class, we played with such business simulations, substituting different variables and seeing how the changes affected the business. We commissioned a team at Intel to put together our pricing and volume models of the PC market and got some very useful and interesting data out of it. In our design of very complex microprocessors, we rely on computer simulations of the chip long before the chip is actually built, to understand its performance and behavior. As computers become more powerful and affordable, I think business simulations will become more commonplace and useful for helping managers think through different scenarios.

"Principle-Centered Leadership" was led by David Hanna of the Covey Leadership Center and was based on a well-known book by Stephen Covey, *The Seven Habits of Highly Effective People*.[23] One interesting exercise was to have your boss, peers, and subordinates evaluate your performance in the seven areas described in Covey's book, and then compare them with your evaluation of yourself. We all did this and looked at the results. We discovered that one's view of oneself tends to be better than others' view of him! This is dangerous, as it leads you to think you're doing better than other people think you are, thus preventing you from taking actions to improve as much as you should.

These were useful inputs for every one of us. As a result of this exercise, I decided to get more frequent feedback from my subordinates in every review I gave them, in addition to the annual review I receive from my boss. I also decided to expand the inputs for my reviews of subordinates. I now solicit feedback from an individual's subordinates and peers to incorporate into my review of that person. This gives me a much more well-rounded picture. The GMs started doing the same. By 1994, all executive staff members at Intel adopted this new policy for performance review.

"External Communications" by Andy Grove was a hands-on session dealing with how to communicate with the press, financial analysts, industry opinion leaders, and the public. Andy began by posing a hypothetical disaster-scenario for a company: dropping orders, poor profits, major competition, you name it. He had each of us prepare and deliver a presentation to the press, industry analysts, and TV news crews. A camera crew recorded our presentations for later playback. He also brought in several people from Intel's Public Relations department, who acted as the audience and asked a whole bunch of hard questions. The whole session was tough but fun! Most of us were sweating through our presentations. After each presentation, Andy played the tape back and analyzed what was good and what needed improvement. The instant feedback was just great and helped us all learn a tremendous amount.

At the end of the session Andy shared his personal experiences and observations on how to communicate effectively with people outside the company. The principles were basically the same as those involved in delivering a good talk, with a few exceptions. He emphasized the need to know the audiences and their concerns. Financial analysts want to know how healthy our business is and our future business outlook. Technology analysts want to know what new products and technologies we are developing. We must relate to our audience right from the beginning and make them feel we understand them and speak their language. Andy also emphasized the need to be clear about the important message we want to convey and, if necessary, repeat it several times. We should come up with sound bites that are simple, quotable, and memorable. For example, saying "The PC will become the most important interactive device on the information highway," is too long and difficult to remember. Andy's sound bite, "The PC is IT," was simple and memorable. Because people have short attention spans, it is easier to remember short sound bites than complicated explanations. So that's what you give them. Andy emphasized the need to be well prepared and think through all the tough questions that are likely to come up. Because most of the GMs attending this session had little previous public exposure, this session was one of the most valuable.

By the summer of 1992, the first GM seminar came to a close. We had a graduation ceremony with a dinner, and gave each participant a diploma and a special pen, certifying that they had become a real GM. The reaction to the whole seminar was overwhelmingly positive. In addition to acquiring some knowledge that translated into tangible actions, the group developed tremendous team spirit and close personal friendships. All of the participants wanted to continue their GM education, so we organized a second GM seminar that began in October of 1992. The topics were:

Strategy II: *Case Studies of Coke and Apple*—David Yoffie
Competitive Forces—Charles Ferguson[24]
Successful Product Case: HP Printers
On-time Shipments: Federal Express
Consumer Electronics—Avram Miller, Intel VP of Business Development

From 1991 to 1993, GM seminars I and II covered a broad spectrum of topics. At the same time, the team members were becoming seasoned GMs. We cannot think of a better way to grow GMs than by learning on the job and participating in ongoing seminars. Since then, Hans Geyer returned to Europe and is now the GM of Intel Europe. Pat Gelsinger moved on to head up the Personal Communications Division, producing Intel Proshare conferencing products, and was subsequently elevated to be vice president of the Business Platform Group. Ron Smith was made vice president of our Computer Enhancements Group in Chandler, Arizona. Several others stayed on to drive our microprocessor business to new heights. Both Peter

Senge and Stephen Covey have become well-known management gurus in their respective areas. HP, Federal Express, Wal-Mart, and Crown continue to do well. There is no question that the PC is becoming the star of digital consumer electronics, as it is moving into the center of digital imaging and digital TV, as predicted in Avram Miller's talk.

When Andy took on the job of CEO in 1987, he shifted his focus from running the operation to driving the corporate strategy. He has done an excellent job. Many people at Intel requested that he teach an internal class on strategies, similar to classes he has conducted on strategy at the Stanford Business School. In February 1994, he started a class at Intel called "Strategy and Action in the Information Processing Industry," with Professor Robert Burgelman of Stanford. The key word here is "action," as strategy is nothing if not acted on. Thinking alone is not strategy—thinking, then acting, is strategy.

Andy picked 25 senior Intel managers to participate in his first class, including eight participants who had completed the GM I and II seminars. The class, team-taught by Andy and Robert, consisted of a series of case studies each lasting two hours, every week for eight weeks. That was not enough time, really, but we were constrained by the difficulties of getting everyone to meet face to face for these interactive sessions, because more than a third of the people came from outside of Santa Clara. We looked at Intel's own memory business, Motorola's communications business, MIPS's microprocessor strategy, IBM's transformation, Apple's strategy, Microsoft's experience in networking, and at the telecom industry. We examined each case in detail, then discussed how to apply what we learned to Intel.

We learned a great deal from this class, but three items stood out. First, watch out for signs of strategic dissonance: is what we do consistent with what we say? Are we allocating resources consistent with our strategy? If not, they should be aligned quickly. In the case of Intel, our massive investment in memories in the early 1980s was in conflict with our shrinking memory business. This strategic dissonance was resolved by nothing short of Intel's momentous decision to get out of the memory business and focus on microprocessors.

Second, compete where you can win and not just for the sake of competing. Motorola competed unsuccessfully with the Japanese across a broad front, although Motorola did not have any particular competitive advantage across this broad front. Often, it is better to identify a battlefield where you can win, rather than continue to fight a losing battle on an old battlefield. Motorola eventually won with cellular phones, an area in which they had competitive strength and advantages.

Third, an alliance is never a substitute for a weak business strategy. It should be a good supplement to a strong strategy. Forming and managing alliances takes a tremendous amount of management time, and you must do it only to support a clear business strategy. Otherwise, the drain will distract management from attending to the core business.

This strategy class has since been repeated several times at different sites, giving many senior managers at Intel an opportunity to participate in learning how to set and then act on strategy.

BUILD A CONTINUOUSLY LEARNING ORGANIZATION

As I outlined before, learning and training are vitally important at our company. The Intel University offers a wide range of management and technical courses for employees. We have special series such as the one for general managers and the strategic management seminars. And every employee is daily involved in rigorous, nonstop, on-the-job training.

In 1994, the Pentium processor was ramping into the marketplace nicely, and several teams were developing next-generation microprocessors in parallel at five different sites. We felt that our teams could accelerate the development process even more by making continuous organizational learning truly a way of life. When a special team analyzed how we might improve on what we were doing, we found that more than 60 percent of the problems we faced had actually been encountered and solved earlier by another team! It occurred to us that if every person knew about or had access to the "best known methods" of other groups at Intel, we could eliminate or dramatically reduce repeat errors and thus improve the overall development process. This would allow each team to innovate on top of the best knowledge of the whole organization and thereby accelerate the pace of innovation. In fact, there was already strong evidence of this organizational learning in our manufacturing group, which practiced a "copy exactly" methodology in duplicating our best manufacturing processes from one factory to another.

I discussed this idea with a number of people and got a warm reception. As a result, my staff and I launched a group-wide program called D2000, with the express intent of dramatically improving the development process and the ramping of new products by having everyone share the best-known methods (BKMs) and accelerating cross-group learning. The goal of D2000 was, by the year 2000, to reach the target of achieving volume production with the very first design of a product. This would be a big improvement over our practice at the time of requiring several design iterations before releasing a product for production. It would be the ultimate demonstration of "do it right the first time."

One of the first things we did was to put together a database of BKMs and associated experts in each technical area. We used the then-new Mosaic browser from the University of Illinois to allow everyone to access and share the information from networked workstations. Since then we have moved on to using more modern browser software. Getting the whole organization to select, document, and adopt BKMs turned out to be a massive task. We also set up joint engineering management and technical teams across all the organizations to make sure the infrastructure for sharing BKMs and learning continuously was in place. There was resistance, as people were afraid that the extensive cross-organizational interactions would slow down innovation. Fortunately, the program began to

FIGURE 15   NEW PRODUCT SHIPMENT FROM BEGINNING OF PRODUCTION

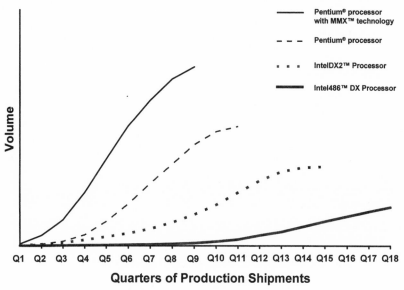

Source: Intel

prove itself very quickly, as we eliminated lots of wasted effort and saw improved teamwork that enabled new products to ramp much faster. As Figure 15 shows, the D2000 program has resulted in accelerating our new product ramp by almost a factor of two since 1994.

This is an ongoing program with just about everybody in the organization involved. We are on track for accomplishing our goal of starting the production ramp on the very first design of a product by around the turn of the century.

In the fast-moving high-technology field, individuals and organizations must keep learning or they will fall behind. Many individuals thrive on learning new skills in either technical or management fields. We work hard to keep learning on a constant basis as a team. We encourage people to learn from each other and share the best known methods. We learn from our successes as well as our failures. And of course we learn from our customers and our competitors.

CHAPTER TWELVE

THE BEST IS YET TO COME

THE PENTIUM PRO PROCESSOR, THE FIRST MEMBER OF THE P6 FAMILY, WAS introduced in 1995 and became a very popular product. But we have to do better. It is time to move on to the next round and have a product that will be the volume microprocessor until the turn of the century, making our older Pentium processor obsolete. At the same time, we must prepare ourselves to make Micro 2011 a reality.

THE PENTIUM II PROCESSOR

We put all our collective learning into building the best possible next-generation microprocessor: the Pentium II processor. It had the same P6 core as the Pentium processor but it was designed on the next generation of silicon technology. Mike Fister, general manager of Microprocessor Divison 6, led the team to incorporate the best architectural and design features into this product. It was designed for high volume and low cost. We developed the chip sets, the motherboard, and other key components to fully support this new product. We worked with all our customers and complementors to build the complementary hardware and software products and the necessary infrastructure. Our extensive program management function brought all the pieces in synch, from design to mass production to marketing promotions.

Because the market for the PC is really worldwide, we launched the

Pentium II processor throughout the world simultaneously from May 5 to 7, 1997. All the key OEM customers and ISV suppliers participated with us in these events. We introduced the complete product, OEMs introduced their new PC systems incorporating the new processor, and ISVs demonstrated leading-edge software products that showed off the power of the systems. All of us brought our newest and best offerings to computer users. It was a collaborative effort in a living ecosystem.

The Pentium II processor has many innovative features that may very well change the shape of personal computing. It incorporates a number of key technologies such as Dynamic Execution technology to deliver blazingly fast general-purpose computing, MMX™ technology to enable great multimedia performance, and the Dual Independent Bus to triple the system bandwidth over previous-generation systems. The combination of these new capabilities delivers the highest performance levels yet to personal computer users. Because of the higher speeds involved between the processor core and the level-two cache, we invented a new form-factor called the single-edge connector cartridge (SECC) that puts the processor core and the cache within a single cartridge. This makes it much easier for our OEM customers to install the processor on the motherboard.

We have a full line of products from the high end of the price point all the way down to the volume PC below $1,000. The combination of the Pentium II processor with the next-generation PCI chip set ushers in the next generation in PC architecture that, we hope, will be the mainstream platform for the rest of the decade. As expected, we face lots of aggressively competing products in the marketplace. The high-technology market is as competitive and vibrant as ever. The beneficiaries are the PC users who will enjoy more and more computing power at lower and lower prices.

MAKING THE DIGITAL FUTURE HAPPEN

As exciting as the projection is for future digital technology, such as the Micro 2011 that was discussed in Chapter 2, it's still only a pro-

FIGURE 16   PENTIUM II PROCESSOR

Source: Intel

jection. None of us knows today how to solve the many technical problems that we need to in order to realize the Micro 2011, just as none of us knew in 1989 how to design a Pentium II processor. How will we cram a billion transistors onto a single chip? How will we manage the heat generated while pushing performance? How will we make sure that the chip is operating 100 percent correctly and provide 100 percent software compatibility? What key features of the chip will enable the most exciting applications?

In 1995, we decided we must start doing longer-term research beyond what we do in product development to get ourselves ready to build the Micro 2011. We must devote resources to looking years down the road in computer architecture, advanced applications, design science, and other key technology areas. In July of 1995, we asked Richard Wirt to start up the Intel Microcomputer Research Labs. We gave him and his team the charter to develop new technologies and build prototypes of future computing products. Richard has done pioneering work on getting optimized operating systems and software to work best on Intel microprocessors. He is the right person to lead the charge.

Richard and I visited research laboratories at IBM, Xerox, Hewlett-Packard, and other companies, as well as many leading universities, to gather ideas on how to run a successful research organization. Everybody that we talked to was extremely open and helpful, and we learned a great deal. We also talked to many of our own people to gather their inputs and ideas. We have since developed our own unique way to run our research labs. We want to do leading-edge research but we also want to harvest research results into our products quickly and efficiently. My earlier experience at Fairchild R&D was a good lesson for us. We did some outstanding research work on semiconductor technology and devices at Fairchild R&D, but unfortunately we had lots of trouble transferring new technology into manufacturing. The R&D lab in Palo Alto and the product groups in Mountain View were less than 10 miles apart, but the cultural separation was huge. Many of us were very frustrated with our lack of success at getting our work from the lab into the marketplace. Andy Grove and Gordon Moore encountered similar obstacles, which was one of the key reasons they left Fairchild to form Intel. One lesson we learned from our Fairchild days was to do our process development work at Intel directly in the production area, to eliminate the gap between development and production. At Intel, development people work side by side with production people and intimately understand each others' issues. Co-locating the research groups with the products groups in the same building allows informal hallway exchanges of ideas on an ongoing basis. When product people hear about research results it stimulates them to think about the future, not only about the task at hand. Research people can learn about the down-to-earth requirements for high-volume products that help shape their research direction. In addition to informal exchanges, the research lab organizes a yearly two-day "show and tell" with lectures and prototype demonstrations of research results open to all product development people. These draw overflowing and enthusiastic crowds.

Today, we have over a hundred talented researchers who are physically co-located with the Intel products groups at three Intel sites. They work closely with the product development groups and also with faculty and students at leading universities on many exciting projects. They are exploring the next round of major applications in networked computing that require huge amounts of computing power. Our research teams are pushing the frontiers of computer architecture and software compilers that may boost microprocessor performance as much as a hundredfold. One group focuses on developing the technologies for coming generations of visual computing. Others are looking at how to design products when the silicon dimensions fall below one tenth of a micron (one micron is one millionth of a meter). Intel's research labs conduct four to five technology forums a year, bringing in leading experts around the world to work with us. We are counting on a close collaboration between research teams and product groups to invent the future of computing and make the exciting Micro 2011 happen.

Inventing high technology is both a technical and a business challenge. We have been blessed with the miracle of silicon technology, which keeps getting better and faster as the dimensions get smaller. The whole high-technology business is built on the silicon foundation. On the human side, we are fortunate to have more and more people around the world entering high technology and contributing to making it an even more exciting business than it is today. It is exhilarating to work with and learn from the best minds around the world and to create the digital future together.

There are tremendous amounts of technological and managerial innovation happening around the world today. The free flow of ideas and the risk-taking culture have been pervasive beyond Intel and the Silicon Valley. They are spreading like wildflowers to all parts of the world. New classes of applications are opening up, which will stimulate even more

exciting innovations and advances in the digital world. What does the digital future look like? Many people ask, "Are we approaching the limits of technology?" "Is innovation slowing down?" "How can there be anything more exciting than the super Pentium II processor?" The digital revolution is still in its early phase. We haven't seen anything yet. The best is yet to come!

A P P E N D I X :
I N T E L   C H R O N O L O G Y

YEAR	INTEL KEY PRODUCTS	KEY EVENTS
1968		Intel founded
1969	3101, first bipolar memory 1101, first CMOS memory	
1970	1103, first dynamic memory	
1971	4004, first 4-bit microprocessor 1702, first EPROM (erasable memory)	Intel went public
1972	8008, fist 8-bit microprocessor	
1974	8080, first 8-bit microprocessor for computing	
1976	8085, integrated 8-bit microprocessor	
1978	8086, first 16-bit microprocessor	
1979	8088, low-cost 16-bit processor	
1981	iAPX 432, high-end 32-bit microprocessor	IBM announced PC with 8088 processor and DOS
1982	80286, 16-bit microprocessor with memory management	

YEAR	INTEL KEY PRODUCTS	KEY EVENTS
1985	386 volume 32-bit processor	Intel exited memory business to focus on microprocessors
1986		Compaq announces first 386 PC
1989	486: 32-bit microprocessor with integrated cache memory and floating point processor 860:32-bit RISC processor	
1990		Intel launched "Red-X" campaign Microsoft announces Windows 3.0
1991		Intel launches "Intel Inside" campaign
1992	486 DX2: first processor with clock-doubling technology PCI chip set	
1993	Pentium processor: superscalar technology	Microsoft announces Windows NT
1995	Pentium Pro processor: Dynamic Execution and Dual Independent Bus	Microsoft announces Windows 95
1996		25th anniversary of the microprocessor
1997	Pentium processor with MMX™ technology Pentium II processor: Dynamic Execution, Dual Independent Bus and MMX™ technology 64-bit "EPIC" technology	

1. Intel and Hewlett-Packard collaborated on the development of the 64-bit instruction set technology called EPIC (Explicitly Parallel Instruction Computing).

2. Brent Schlender, "Killer Chip," *Fortune*, November 10, 1997, p. 70.

3. P. Gelsinger, P. Gargini, G. Parker, and A. Yu, "2001: A Microprocessor Odyssey," *Technology 2001* (Derek Leebaert, editor), MIT Press, 1991, p. 95.

4. Gordon Moore, "Cramming More Components Onto Integrated Circuits," *Electronics Magazine* (vol. 38, no. 8), April 19, 1965.

5. Modern interconnects use different alloys of aluminum and copper.

6. Thanks to Richard Wirt and Hen-Wen Wang of Intel for collecting the data.

7. Bits indicates the number of logic data that can be executed at one time. The higher the number, the more powerful is the machine.

8. William Davidow, *Marketing High Technology*, The Free Press, 1986.

9. Bus refers to the set of electrical connections between a microprocessor and the rest of the chips on a board. An 8-bit bus can communicate data 8 bits at a time. A 16-bit bus communicates twice as fast, but is more expensive because there are more connections or pins on the chip.

10. See Chapter 10, "Obsolete Our Own Products."

11. A. S. Grove, *High Output Management*, Random House, 1983; 2nd edition, Vantage Books, 1995.

12. Alfred Sloan, Jr, *My Years with General Motors*, Doubleday & Company, 1963.

13. A motherboard is the main circuit board in a PC, containing the microprocessor, the memory, and other support chips.

14. First used by A. M. Brandenburger and B. J. Nalebuff, "The Right Game: Use Game Theory to Shape Strategy," *Harvard Business Review*, July/August 1995, p. 60.

15. James F. Moore, *The Death of Competition*, Harper Business, 1996.

16. This error was caused by an erratum in only one of the early Pentium processor versions. This erratum did not exist on other Intel microprocessors such as the 486, Pentium Pro, or Pentium II processors.

17. "Tomorrow's CPU's," *BYTE*, November 1996, p. 76.

18. A term used in Andy Grove's book, *Only the Paranoid Survive*, Currency/Doubleday, 1996.

19. Complementary MOS, which employs two different transistors in a complementary fashion to perform logic functions.

20. Silicon technology is typically characterized by the size of the line width on the chip. One micron is one-millionth of a meter. By way of reference, a human hair is about 100 microns!

21. Paul Hersey, *The Situational Leader*, Warner Books, 1984.

22. Peter Senge, *The Fifth Discipline*, Currency/Doubleday, 1990.

23. Steven Covey, *The Seven Habits of Highly Effective People*, A Fireside Book, Simon & Schuster, 1989.

24. Charles Ferguson and Charles Morris, *Computer Wars*, Times Books, Random House, 1993.

INDEX

ABOUT THE AUTHOR

ALBERT YU IS SENIOR VICE PRESIDENT OF INTEL CORPORATION AND General Manager of the Microprocessor Products Group, responsible for the microprocessors used in most personal computers, such as the Pentium® processor with MMX technology, the Pentium II processor, and future generations of microprocessors such as the Merced processor. He is also responsible for technology developments in microcomputer software, design technology, and microcomputer research laboratories. His group is located at six different sites around the world.

Albert was born in Shanghai, China. He moved with his parents to Taipei, where he attended high school, and later to Hong Kong. He emigrated to the United States and received a B.S. from the California Institute of Technology and M.S. and Ph.D. degrees from Stanford University, all in electrical engineering. He joined Fairchild Semiconductor Laboratory upon graduation from Stanford University and became Director of the Exploratory Devices Department.

Albert joined Intel in 1972 and has taken on a variety of management roles in manufacturing development, reliability engineering, and technology development. He left Intel in 1977 to form a company called VideoBrain, which built the first home computer. He later pioneered the use of microcomputers in China. He returned to Intel in 1981 as Director of Quality and Reliability. In 1984, he joined the Microcomputer Group as Director of Strategic Product Planning and became Assistant General Manager and General Manager of the group. Since 1990, he has been the General Manager of the Microprocessor Products Group of Intel, driving the definition, development, and delivery of the Intel microprocessor products. He has taught many management classes and published over 27 technical and professional papers. He authored a best-selling book in Chinese, *Insider's View of Intel,* published in 1995. He is a board member of Power One. In 1989 he was given the Distinguished Asian Executive Award by the Asian Business League of San Francisco. He serves on advisory councils at Stanford University's Center of Integrated Systems and the University of California at Berkeley's School of Computer Science and Engineering. He is a senior member of the American Leadership Forum in Santa Clara, California; IEEE; and the Computer Society.